LAKE
WHATCOM

LAKE
WHATCOM
· A HISTORY ·

H. LEON GREENE

THE
History
PRESS

Published by The History Press
Charleston, SC
www.historypress.com

Copyright © 2024 by H. Leon Greene
All rights reserved

Back cover, top: White City Amusement Park, circa 1909. *Whatcom Museum, X.6000.747.*

First published 2024

Manufactured in the United States

ISBN 9781467155533

Library of Congress Control Number: 2023950631

CONTENTS

ACKNOWLEDGEMENTS

Special thanks to Ruth Steele and Rozlind Koester at the Center for Pacific Northwest Studies (CPNWS), Alison Costanza at the Washington State Archives Northwest Regional Branch and Jeff Jewell at the Whatcom Museum.

AUTHOR'S NOTE

For simplicity of verbiage, the towns of Whatcom, Sehome, Bellingham and Fairhaven are often collectively called Bellingham, even in descriptions of these cities before their final merger in 1903.

All photographic images have undergone limited cropping for aesthetic purposes.

Abbreviations:

BIERY PAPERS: Galen Biery Papers and Photographs, Center for Pacific Northwest Studies, Heritage Resources, Western Libraries, Western Washington University.

BUSWELL PAPERS: Howard E. Buswell Papers and Photographs, Center for Pacific Northwest Studies, Heritage Resources, Western Libraries, Western Washington University.

CPNWS: Center for Pacific Northwest Studies, Archives and Special Collections, Western Libraries, Western Washington University, Bellingham, Washington.

Chapter 1

LAKE WHATCOM GEOLOGY

Lake Whatcom is integral to the history of Bellingham. About twelve miles long and one mile wide at its widest point and located about three miles from the center of Bellingham, it was formed by glacial erosion and has approximately thirty miles of shoreline. Originally, the smaller Lakes Louise, Cain and Reed were part of Lake Whatcom, but glacial silt separated them from the major body of water. Lake Whatcom is Washington State's fifth-largest freshwater lake by volume, following Lakes Chelan, Washington, Crescent and Ozette. Lake Whatcom has only one island: Reveille Island, with an area of 11.4 acres. Reveille Island had ceremonial significance to the local Native Americans in the 1800s; artifacts discovered there have included pictographs and a stone bowl.

As a recreational paradise, Lake Whatcom provides swimming, boating, sailing, windsurfing, water skiing, canoeing, kayaking and fishing. Lake Whatcom is also the source of drinking water for all of Bellingham and many of the surrounding communities.

The depth of the lake varies from 15 to 334 feet. The lake itself has three distinct regions or basins formed by natural boundaries. The three basins are quite unequal in size and are formed by underwater ridges (sills) that divide the lake into sections. Basin No. 1 (the Silver Beach Basin) extends from the northern part of the lake to approximately Fairview Street in Geneva and the Eagle Ridge development on the other side of the lake. It is separated from Basin No. 2 by the Geneva sill. Basin No. 2 (the Geneva Basin) is bookended by the Geneva sill and the Strawberry sill. The Geneva sill sits only 10 to 15

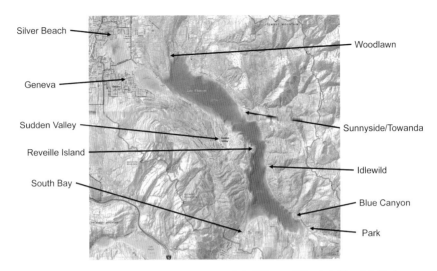

Major settlements and sites around Lake Whatcom. *Lake Whatcom Watershed, City of Bellingham.*

feet below the surface of the water, and the Strawberry sill is a maximum of 42 feet below the surface, averaging 20–30 feet. The Strawberry sill begins at Strawberry Point on the west side and Dellesta Park Drive on the east. Basin No. 3—overwhelmingly the largest—is itself divided into a north basin and a south basin by the Sunnyside sill that is 209 feet below the surface. Basin No. 1 has a maximum depth of 100 feet; Basin No. 2 is 76 feet deep but averages 40–60 feet; North Basin No. 3 is 272 feet deep; and South Basin No. 3 is 334 feet deep.

The lake's surface covers about five thousand acres, and it holds 250 million gallons of water. It is fed by thirty-six streams, seven of which flow year-round: Silver Beach, Anderson, Carpenter, Austin, Olsen, Smith and Brannian Creeks. Only a small proportion of the water in the lake comes from direct precipitation itself. During portions of the year, Lake Whatcom receives water from the Middle Fork of the Nooksack River through a series of tunnels and pipes. The outflow of Lake Whatcom is Whatcom Creek; the volume of flow is adjusted by a small manually controlled dam (construction completed in 1938) at the northwest end of the lake. By regulation, the lake is not allowed to rise more than 314.94 feet above mean sea level. Over the course of the year, the lake level varies by a maximum of only 4 feet. Whatcom Creek delivers its water into Bellingham Bay just south of C Street and Holly Street.

Near Lake Whatcom are three small mountains—Squalicum to the north, Stewart to the northeast and Lookout to the west.

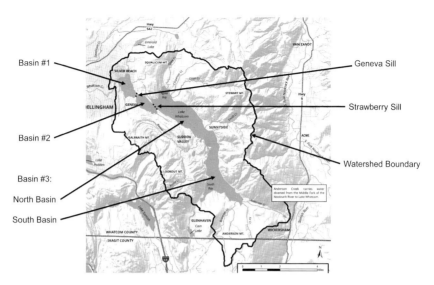

Lake Whatcom watershed and basins. Basin No. 3 is by far the largest of the three. *Stewards of the Lake, Lake Whatcom Management Program, Whatcom County, WA, and the City of Bellingham.*

Lake Whatcom bathymetric map. *Lake Whatcom Bathymetric Map & Profile, City of Bellingham.*

Weather around Lake Whatcom is generally mild; however, over a century ago, extremes were more common. In 1907, the lake froze, with ice up to six inches thick in some places. Steamers on the lake became icebound. Nevertheless, the subsequent summer, the weather was warm enough for nude bathers to congregate.

Looking toward future needs of the population of Bellingham, engineers built a dam on the Middle Fork of the Nooksack River, beginning in 1950; it was not completed until 1961 and not operational until 1962. Water from this source began to flow into Lake Whatcom in 1964. The dam featured a channel that emptied into an eight-foot-diameter tunnel that went under Bowman Mountain for about 1.6 miles, then into a 9.5-mile pipeline to Mirror Lake, emptying into Lake Whatcom via Anderson Creek. The control gates on the Nooksack regulate the amount of water diverted to Lake Whatcom, which varies as Bellingham's needs for water change from month to month. At the time the dam was constructed, little attention was given to the ability of local fish—four or five species of salmon: chinook (king), coho (silver), chum, pink and perhaps sockeye—to spawn in that branch of the river. Trout and steelhead have also been documented there. The dam was reconfigured to allow passage of spawning fish, a project that was approved in 2019 and substantially completed in 2021.

Chapter 2

NATIVE AMERICAN ROOTS

Mapping of the Pacific Northwest region was accomplished by many explorers, such as Juan de Fuca, Manuel Quimper and George Vancouver, but in 1841, Lieutenant Charles Wilkes provided detail about the geography of the entire Puget Sound region. Native Americans had a presence here for centuries before these explorers. Tribes of the Salish tradition included the Samish, the Nooksack and the Lummi, and some are thought to have been here over five thousand years ago, soon after the last ice age. They concentrated around Bellingham Bay and along the Nooksack River and its branches.

The name Whatcom derives from the Nooksack word meaning "noisy (or rumbling) waters," describing the scene around the Whatcom Creek as it emptied into Bellingham Bay at the lower waterfalls. Whatcom was also the name of a Nooksack chief.

The Lummi predominated at the mouth of Whatcom Creek where it flowed into Bellingham Bay. However, they had no permanent settlement there, occupying the region only during the warmer months. Their settlement on the Nooksack River was a site called the Portage, and trails led to the northeast to the Saquantch and the Nooksack (the Sumas region today) and southeast to the Neuk-wers of the Stick Samish or Sia-mannas (the southern end of Lake Whatcom). The village on Lake Whatcom was called Kaw-tcha-a-ha-meek, located at the southern end of the lake on the trail to the South Fork of the Nooksack; it was an important camping ground.

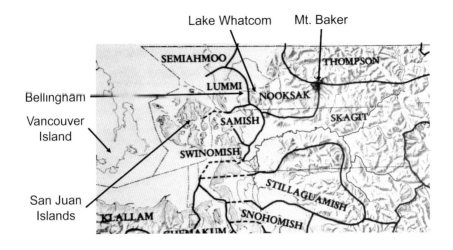

Native American tribal lands, circa 1820. *Adapted from map 11 in James W. Scott and Roland L. Delorme,* Historical Atlas of Washington *(Norman: University of Oklahoma Press, 1988).*

A northwest coast Salish tribe (the Saquantch) was said to occupy the south end of Lake Whatcom. A Salish map named the village there hahch-wah-AHM-eck. Another phonetic spelling: Kaw-tcha-ha-muk or Kaw-tchaa-ha-muk. The occupants of this village may have been either Nooksack or Stick Samish or both. This Saquantch tribe was later defeated and replaced by the Lummi in about 1800. The Saquantch thereafter moved farther inland. Native Americans in the Whatcom County region had cultural and linguistic similarities to the tribes farther north in Canada and Vancouver Island, the Saanich First Nation, in particular.

All these tribes depended on fishing, shellfish and wild game for their survival. They additionally harvested roots, berries and local fruits and vegetables. Lumbering was important, with cedar especially prominent in the construction of their houses, meeting places and boats.

On December 14 or 15, 1852, Captain Henry Roeder and Russell Peabody came to Bellingham Bay and established the first White settlement in the area. Washington Territory was formed on March 2, 1853. Whatcom County itself was created on March 9, 1854, by parceling off the northern portion of what was then Island County. Having a larger north–south dimension than today's Whatcom County, it covered land from the Canadian border including today's Whatcom and Skagit Counties where it met the then-smaller Island County (King County was the entity just south of Island County). Whatcom County in 1854 encompassed all of today's Whatcom,

Skagit, San Juan and Island Counties. Washington would become a state on November 11, 1889.

The arrival of non-Native populations brought with it the introduction of diseases. Smallpox and other contagious illnesses decimated the Native American population, by some estimates decreasing it by 90 percent.

An early report from the Bureau of Indian Affairs in 1857 was one of the first detailed descriptions of the Indian population around Bellingham Bay. Special Indian Agent E.C. Fitzhugh reported that there were five tribes in the area, and he estimated the numbers of each:

Neuk-sack: 450

Samish: 150

Lummis: 510

Neuk-wers and Sia-man-nas (who were also called the Stick Indians or Stick Samish): 200 in total.

Fitzhugh called the Neuk-sack, Samish and Lummi tribes the Salt Indians, for their more common location on the salt water of Bellingham Bay.

The Neuk-sacks (Nooksacks) lived toward the interior near Mount Baker, close to today's Lynden, Maple Falls and Goshen, and apparently they interacted only reluctantly with the White man. Their major crop was potatoes, which they traded with White men for clothes. Fish was a large part of their diet, mostly salmon and shellfish. They also caught trout and sturgeon and hunted for elk and deer. The Indian agents often traded or gave items to the Neuk-sacks: tobacco, pipes, buttons, thread, shirts and occasionally blankets. At least by 1857, diseases had not yet been imported into the Neuk-sack tribe by the White men. The Nuek-sacks were described as strong and athletic. They had three distinct groups, and all recognized Hump-klam as their chief. The lower band of the Neuk-sacks resided about six miles from Lake Whatcom. The name Neuk-sack meant "mountain men." This tribe had no slaves, and the men had but one wife.

The Samish were described by Fitzhugh as "more of a wandering class," inhabiting both bay islands and the coastal inland. Fishing was their major activity. They had previously been much more populous, numbering about two thousand only ten to twelve years earlier, but warring tribes from the north had decimated their numbers.

The Lummis were divided into three groups, one each at the mouths of the three entries of the Lummi River into the bay, along the coastline from Point Whitehorn at the south end of Birch Bay to Chuckanut Bay; some also lived in the San Juan Islands. All recognized Chow-ate-sot as their chief. Like the Samish, they had been more numerous in past years but had been ravaged by northern tribes. Superstitious, they believed that when they died, they would be reincarnated as birds or animals. They specifically refused to eat pheasants or owls for this reason, though it is unclear why eating other animals was acceptable.

The Neuk-wers (also spelled Nux^w a ha) and the Sia-man-nas (Samish) lived, as described by Fitzhugh, "in the back country on the lake and streams adjacent" around Lake Whatcom and Lake Sia-man-na (Samish) and the rivers that drained into them, specifically the southwestern shore of Lake Whatcom. They had little contact with the other tribes, which tended toward the coast, and they did not encounter a White man until about 1853. Describing the Indians living around Lake Whatcom, Fitzhugh said, "They dress in skins and blankets, made of dogs' hair and feathers, of their own manufacture. They have had no muskets until the last three years. They cultivate small patches of potatoes, but subsist principally on elk, deer, and fish and dried berries."

Another tribe, the Sem-mi-an-mas (Semiahmoos), lived both inland and on the far northern coast of the territory near present-day Blaine. They had also suffered from raids by northern Indians, and by 1857, their numbers had dwindled to about one hundred total. Potatoes were their main staple.

The Skagit tribe lived slightly farther south.

The more northern Indians along the Canadian border frequently traded with the Hudson Bay Company.

Some reports claim that an area around Lake Whatcom was off-limits or taboo to some of the Indian tribes. While nearby burial grounds might have contributed to this sense of a sacred prohibition against occupation of the land, it's unclear if this was actually the reason. Reveille Island has always had this sort of tradition associated with it, though actual burial grounds have never been found there. Another legend had an Indian chief named Altama and his wife, Anola, jumping off a cliff on the eastern side of Reveille Island into the water below to avoid capture or murder by a northern tribe. Unusual music reported coming from the ghosts of those deceased on Reveille Island may have been wind or water echoing through rocks along the coast of the island.

Chapter 3

FIRST BELLINGHAM SETTLERS

Juan de Fuca, a Greek whose given name was Apóstolos Valerianos, came to the Pacific Northwest region in about 1592 under the sponsorship of King Philip II of Spain. Other Spanish explorers, including Manuel Quimper, saw Bellingham Bay in 1792, close to the time that Mount Baker last erupted, in July 1792. Mount Baker had been originally called La Gran Montaña del Carmelo by the Spanish, but it was later renamed Mount Baker by men exploring with the British George Vancouver, also in 1792. This same Spanish group initially named the bay the Golfo de Gaston, but Vancouver would later rename it Bellingham Bay after Sir William Bellingham, the British navy provisioner for the Vancouver expedition and controller of storekeepers' accounts for the British navy.

Simon Fraser with the North West Company—fur traders—came to the Strait of Georgia on August 8, 1808. This opened the region to development through trading along the upper Pacific lands. In 1821, the Hudson's Bay Company merged with the North West Company, and in 1825 it opened the first trading post in the region that would become Whatcom County. A man named William Jarman, known as Blanket Bill, came to what would be Whatcom County as perhaps the first White settler in the region with his Native American wife, homesteading near the mouth of Friday Creek.

Henry Roeder and Russell V. Peabody, both ship's captains, had been unsuccessful seeking their fortune in gold in the West. The fire in San Francisco in 1851 suddenly created a market for timber to rebuild the city, so farther north, they sought a source of lumber to harvest and sell. Traveling to what is now the Port Townsend region of Washington, they met up with William Pattle, who told them that some local Native Americans had described to him a region farther north at Bellingham Bay that had abundant timber, a creek to provide waterpower and coal. Pattle told Roeder and Peabody that he would show them where it was for $1,000. They declined and, on their own, engaged a Native American Salish Lummi guide for $1 per day. This guide—and perhaps a few others—brought them by canoe with four to six other men to Bellingham Bay, traditionally dated December 14, 1852. They were introduced to Chow-ate-sot (also rendered Chow'it'sut or Chowitzet), the chief of the Lummi tribe (also then called the Flathead tribe). The chief granted Roeder and Peabody access to this region, showed them the creek that would be the source of power for the lumber mill (Whatcom Creek where it emptied into Bellingham Bay), allegedly gave them ownership of the land and even helped them begin their venture of selling timber—mostly red cedar and Douglas fir. Soon thereafter, Edward Eldridge came to the site in 1853, along with his wife, Teresa, the first White woman to settle in the area (she was later known as the "mother of Whatcom"). Chow-ate-sot went on to grant further ownership of both Lummi and Nooksack lands to the White man at the Treaty of Point Elliott in 1855 (ratified in 1859).

Just before the lumbering began, William Pattle discovered coal about one and a half to two miles south of the site of the Roeder lumber mill. Pattle had also been lumbering on the San Juan Islands, supplying timber to San Francisco. Some Native Americans of the Lummi tribe told him that "black fire dirt" was present on Bellingham Bay, so he went there and discovered an outcropping of coal near what would later be known as Fairhaven. In the process, Pattle founded Unionville, a town that was to become Bellingham and Fairhaven. Pattle opened his coal mine near where the Chrysalis Inn is located today; however, it never produced any significant amount of coal. The Pattle mine was abandoned in 1855.

Roeder and Peabody quickly established their lumber mill, and by the fall of 1853, they were shipping their product locally and down the West Coast. However, by 1854, their lumber venture had begun to fail. The summer of 1853 was hot and dry, and the waterpower from Whatcom Creek emptying out of Lake Whatcom was insufficient for cutting sufficient numbers of logs. Furthermore, the price of lumber had fallen from its high following the San Francisco fire. At about this same time, Roeder and Peabody each took a donation claim of 160 acres in the area where Sehome would be later located. (The final demise of the lumber mill would come in 1873, when it burned.) Roeder briefly returned to seafaring pursuits.

At nearly the same time in 1854 (some reports say 1853), another miner, William Brown, along with Henry Hewitt, similarly discovered coal while working for Roeder and Peabody's lumber mill. This deposit was located at the base of Sehome Hill, exposed by an uprooted tree, not far from the Pattle mine. Brown and Hewitt began work there under the name Sehome Mine, calling their new company the Bellingham Bay Coal Company. The mine was quite productive in its first year, reportedly clearing a profit of $300,000. The Sehome Mine continued until about 1878, when it was closed.

By 1854, the towns of Fairhaven, Bellingham, Sehome and Whatcom had been started, all small and very close to one another. The territorial legislature declared this area to be the Whatcom county seat. Each town would have its own distinctive character. Whatcom began as a timber exporter that later also saw railroads in its future; Sehome was to be a coal-producing town; Bellingham, likewise, had visions of coal mines; and Fairhaven would eventually imagine itself as a terminus for the transcontinental railroad.

The Donation Land Claim Act of 1850 was responsible for some of the impetus for settlement around Lake Whatcom. This law provided 640 acres to each married couple and 320 acres to any single person who had resided in Oregon Territory prior to December 1, 1850. Claimants were required to work the land for four consecutive years to finalize the grant. Those who arrived in the territory between December 1, 1850, and December 1, 1853, could claim half that amount of land. The majority of the settlement around Lake Whatcom occurred later, however. In 1862, President Lincoln signed the Homestead Act, which granted 160 acres to heads of families who devoted five years of continuous residence and improvements on a plot of land already surveyed. This land could be claimed by citizens or those working toward citizenship, and a small monetary fee was required to compete the deed transfer.

A non–Native American land claim in the Lake Whatcom region was filed as early as June 23, 1858, by William Dermiston and J.B. Lascomb, but by 1864, only five claims existed on the west side of the lake and only seven on the east side. The lack of adequate roads was likely responsible for the dearth of settlers. Travel from Bellingham Bay to Lake Whatcom remained difficult through the late 1800s. The entire trip could take one or two days. Furthermore, the land to the north around Lynden and Sumas was more amenable to farming. Land claims burgeoned around 1890, and by 1899 all land encircling Lake Whatcom had a person's name attached to it. Turnover was rapid. Many owners sold their holdings to logging companies. The timber around the lake was dense, and conventional farming was difficult because clearing the land required much work. Old-growth Douglas fir tree stumps could be next to impossible to remove.

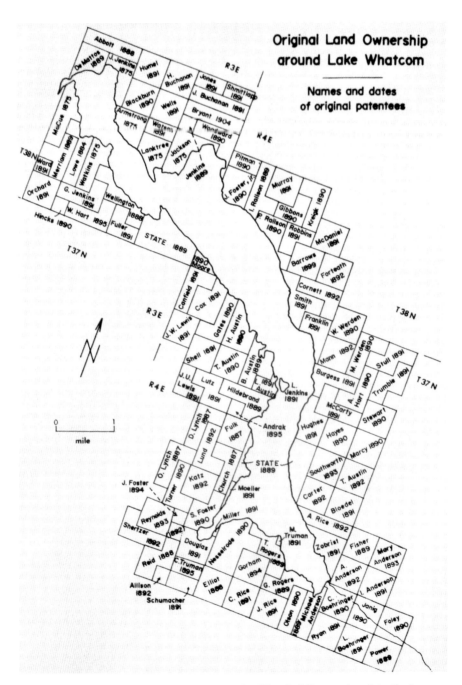

Early land claims around Lake Whatcom. *From* An Historical Geography of the Settlement Around Lake Whatcom Prior to 1920, *F. Stanley Moore, Pamphlet Collection, 1857–2003, CP.NWS.*

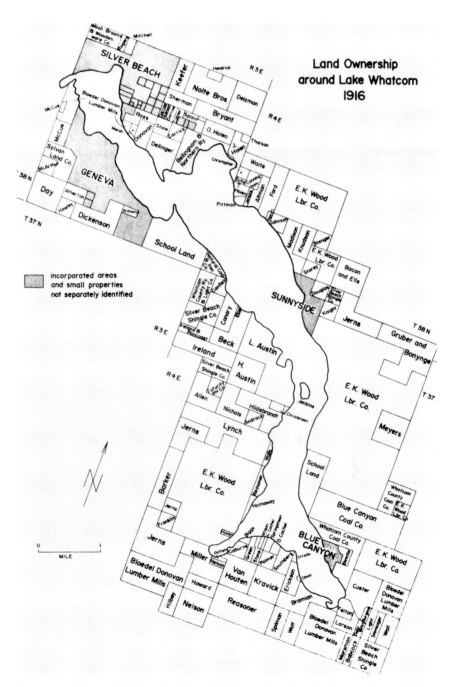

Land ownership by 1916. *From* An Historical Geography of the Settlement Around Lake Whatcom Prior to 1920, *F. Stanley Moore, Pamphlet Collection, 1857–2003, CP.NWS.*

In 1856, the United States Army established Fort Bellingham, located where the Smith Gardens now occupy Marine Drive, about three miles northwest of the largest coal mines and lumber mills. The fort was designed to protect settlers from local Native Americans, and Captain George Pickett (of Pickett's Charge fame during the Civil War) was in command of this outpost of sixty men. The discovery of gold in the British Columbia Fraser River Valley in late 1857 or the spring of 1858 caused a brief boom in the population and activity around Bellingham as miners flocked to Bellingham on their way to the gold mines. Almost simultaneously, around August 1858, the gold rush ended as the men discovered that the quantity of the precious metal had been greatly overestimated and it had been completely mined. Bellingham returned to its previous sleepy condition.

Maps of the era often showed towns and roads that existed only in the minds of land speculators and developers. Woodlawn, Lakeview, Idlewild and Sunnyside (Towanda) never materialized at any size, while Geneva, Blue Canyon, Park and Silver Beach were birthed and, at least briefly, survived. Some grew and then dwindled; Blue Canyon was a town of about one thousand souls at its peak, slowly shrinking as the coal mining boom evaporated.

Early roads were primitive. The first went to what would be the Silver Beach area in about 1864. It was hardly more than a crude trail and would not be sufficient for transporting coal and timber to Bellingham Bay. Roads were dusty and irregular in the dry season but nearly impassable during rainy months. Travel to Geneva required a trip first from Bellingham (then the complex of Whatcom, Sehome, Bellingham and Fairhaven) to Silver Beach on that primitive trail, then by boat to Echo Point (now called Strawberry Point) and subsequently on foot or horseback via a trail to Geneva. The early boats were small man-powered craft or sailboats, though wind power on the lake was unreliable.

A trail was also blazed from the Sehome area to Geneva in the mid-1860s. "Dirty" Dan Harris singlehandedly improved this trail into a semi-useful road to Lake Whatcom in October 1875 for $300. It followed roughly the route taken by today's Lakeway Drive, a distance of three to four miles. It sufficed as a route to the lake until E.F.G. Carlyon improved the road to Silver Beach along today's Alabama Street in the late 1880s. A road from the south end of Lake Whatcom to Alger did not appear until 1906.

Boats began to proliferate as soon as coal mining, and then timbering, were developed. Boats were used for passengers, supplies, mail and, eventually, for coal, timber and shingles.

Chapter 4

BELLINGHAM, THE MERGER OF FOUR CITIES

W hat we now call Bellingham began as four small towns within a short distance of each other: Whatcom, Sehome, Bellingham (originally called Unionville) and Fairhaven. They would soon find themselves formally platted and competing. Whatcom, on the north, was platted in July 1858; Sehome, next to the east and south, was platted in May 1858; Bellingham, still farther to the south, was platted in 1871, and Fairhaven, the southernmost town, was platted in 1883. Furthermore, the area around Lake Whatcom began to see settlers. During this entire time, the residents around Bellingham Bay dreamed that their towns would become a major terminus for one of the transcontinental railroads making their way across the United States.

It made sense for the four small towns to merge. The planning for electricity, water, trolleys and other services would be simplified if the four towns were a single entity. But local pride inhibited mergers. Fairhaven magnates essentially bought the city of Bellingham in 1890. Whatcom and Sehome joined forces in 1891 and adopted the name New Whatcom. As early as the mid-1890s, local politicians devised a plan to merge the four towns. It failed. The word "New" was dropped from the name "New Whatcom" in 1901. But Whatcom and Fairhaven resisted further merger, in part simply because of the name—Fairhaven did not want to become Whatcom, and Whatcom did not want to become Fairhaven. Finally, the compromise was to revert to the use of the name Bellingham, the smallest

Four towns
competed for
dominance at
Bellingham
Bay: Fairhaven,
Bellingham,
Sehome and
Whatcom.
*Whitney's Map of the
Bellingham Bay Cities
and Environs, compiled
by Edmund S. Hincks,
Whatcom Museum,
1995.0015.000007.*

of the four towns. The vote on October 27, 1903, for the official merger of
the cities passed, 2163 to 596. The merger was approved on November 4,
1903, and on December 28, 1903, the deal was finalized as the new mayor
and city council took office. This new town of Bellingham would soon
become totally dependent on Lake Whatcom for its survival.

Chapter 5

TITANS OF LAKE WHATCOM

John Joseph Donovan

John J. Donovan was almost synonymous with the city of Bellingham in the late 1800s and early 1900s. He was trusted above any other businessman in the development of Whatcom County, and his influence cannot be overstated.

Donovan's family originated in the southern portion of Ireland, coming to the United States in the mid-1800s. Greatly influenced by the impact of the Irish potato famine, the Donovan family was determined to send as many of its members as possible to the United States as immigrants. JJ, as he was often called, was born on September 8, 1858, and began his education in Plymouth, New Hampshire. By age thirteen, he had started the habit of keeping detailed diaries, usually one book for each year. These would later prove invaluable in tracking his life history. The young Donovan pursued farm work and sports, especially bicycling. He entered the Plymouth Normal School (now Plymouth State University) in 1875, and there he met Clara Isabel Nichols ("Nickie") from Melrose, Massachusetts. Donovan graduated in 1877, after which he taught school for about three years in New Hampshire and Massachusetts. He enrolled in what is now Worcester Polytechnic Institute in 1880, graduating as valedictorian in 1882 and becoming a civil engineer in Worcester, Massachusetts. At graduation, Donovan joined the Northern Pacific Railway Company, where he would work from 1882 to 1891. He advanced rapidly and cemented his connection to railroads, grand projects and large business ventures. Donovan soon thereafter engineered some important railroad bridges, and he quickly transferred to the Cascade Division of the Northern Pacific, where he helped complete the connection across Washington Territory to the West Coast, which included boring a tunnel, completed in June 1887, through the Cascades at Stampede Pass toward a terminus at Tacoma. Donovan came to Fairhaven in December 1888 to work for Nelson Bennett, initially with the goal of constructing a railroad to bring coal from Skagit County to the port in Bellingham.

J.J. Donovan, circa 1890. *Biery Papers, #0228, CPNWS.*

John and Clara had an extended courtship during this time, lasting nearly twelve years. Clara had become a piano instructor in Melrose, Massachusetts. On the surface, they were quite different; he was the son of poor immigrants, a self-made engineer and a Catholic; she was the product of gentrified New England, a teacher and a Protestant. They married on April 29, 1888, in Melrose, Massachusetts; at the time, Donovan was living in Helena, Montana. They would become the parents of three children: Helen Elizabeth Donovan (born 1889), John Nichols Donovan (born 1891) and Philip Laurence Donovan (born 1893). The Donovans would belong to "high society" in Bellingham, if there was even such a designation; they were wealthy by any standards. The family moved to Fairhaven in 1889.

In 1891–92, Donovan was the chief engineer for the new Blue Canyon Coal Mining Company and its railroad connection to the bay, the Bellingham Bay and Eastern Railway. Donovan's connection to the Blue Canyon Coal Mine started with his friendship with James Wardner. Wardner was a promoter, a huckster, a jokester with a good sense of humor and an astute businessman whose riches originated in mining. Wardner had bought the Blue Canyon Mine in 1890; Donovan became the general manager. Quick to buy and sell, Wardner sold his interest in the Blue Canyon Mine in 1891. Many of Donovan's jobs overlapped, as he was engineer and manager for many businesses at the turn of the century.

In the late 1800s, the entire West Coast felt the impact of railroads. During the early years of the development of these railroads, the leaders of Bellingham sought to make it the terminus of one of these lines. In the frenzy to complete transcontinental lines, many cities vied for the placement of a major railroad in their community, but in 1873, the Northern Pacific chose Tacoma, and in 1891, the Great Northern chose Everett. The Northern Pacific came through Stampede Pass, and the Great Northern used Stevens Pass to push its line to Everett. Bellingham was unsuccessful.

In 1898, Donovan became general superintendent and chief engineer of the Bellingham Bay and British Columbia (BB&BC) Railway, and he revived the dreams that Bellingham might become a major connection between transcontinental railways and shipping by sea. Now he was energized to find a new route over the Cascades to Spokane, an extension of the BB&BC Railway from its current dead-end in Glacier. He envisioned it connecting with rails to the rest of the United States from Spokane. Donovan and his exploratory crews labored for three years, trudging along proposed routes to establish the best and cheapest route, but they were unsuccessful. The BB&BC abandoned the project. Donovan would continue to seek funding and support elsewhere for the cross-state railway through 1906, but his efforts went nowhere. On March 31, 1906, Donovan resigned from his position at BB&BC Railway.

By 1898, Donovan had become associated with Julius Bloedel and Peter Larson, and they recognized the potential of the logging and lumber industry, forming the Lake Whatcom Logging Company with Larson as president, Donovan as vice president and Bloedel as manager. Their original holdings were 160 acres of timber at South Bay, Lake Whatcom. Immediately, these three also formed the Larson Lumber Company in an area at the edge of Lake Whatcom that would be known as the town of Larson, today the area encompassed by Bloedel-Donovan Park and the Old Mill Village. The same officers were in charge. Their business there consisted of two mills—named, unimaginatively, Mill A and Mill B, completed in 1907. Soon, the business would have these two large sawmills (plus two shingle mills) on Lake Whatcom and one on Bellingham Bay, acquired from the Bellingham Bay Improvement Company's Cargo Mill, which had been constructed in 1893. It would eventually add a sash and door factory. Their holdings also expanded to an area that contained 1.2 billion feet of timber. Their businesses became the primary employer of the region, giving jobs to an average of over one thousand men (sometimes as many as three thousand). All the while, Donovan also became vice president of the First National Bank of Bellingham.

Donovan was a Catholic, and as such, he promoted many of the local projects of the Catholic Church. He became president of the Catholic

Federation of Washington, and he was a longtime member of the Knights of Columbus. Donovan's staunch Catholic beliefs corresponded to what by today's standards would be called evangelical Catholicism. He also occasionally spoke out about moral issues in the community. Brian Griffin's *Treasures from the Trunk* includes a letter written by Donovan in 1912 that chided Bellingham's Grand Theater for performing songs he deemed "rank and unfit for decent people to hear." Politically, he stood with the Republicans. Even with all his other projects, Donovan promoted education through the development of the Northwest Normal School, founded in 1886 in Lynden, Washington, primarily as a woman's school for training teachers. It would ultimately become Western Washington University.

By April 1913, the two companies—the Lake Whatcom Logging Company and the Larson Lumber Company—had merged, installing Bloedel as president and Donovan as vice president. The company continued to expand, and by 1928, the Bloedel-Donovan Mill was the largest on the West Coast.

There was hardly a major business in Bellingham that didn't feel the touch of J.J. Donovan. The Bellingham Bay Improvement Corporation, the Blue Canyon Coal Mine, the Bellingham Coal Mine, the Larson Lumber Mill, the Bloedel-Donovan Lumber Mill and countless others were influenced by his business acumen.

Donovan was active in many associations of lumbermen, and he was a keen supporter of road development in the state. As an employer, he was kind and generous to his employees, ensuring that they had adequate housing, providing a degree of health insurance and supporting temperance and prohibition. In contrast to the many company towns of the era that cheated and bilked their employees, Donovan supported his workers and was sympathetic to their needs. He ran his businesses with honor and integrity, even boosting company morale with company picnics and social gatherings. He gave generously to charities and was known for his integrity in business dealings. Donovan's gentle character and compassion toward his fellow man were evident.

J.J. Donovan died at age seventy-eight on January 9, 1937, following a three-year illness that was likely a form of dementia. He was buried in Bellingham's Bay View Cemetery.

Julius Harold Bloedel

Julius Harold Bloedel was born in Fond du Lac, Wisconsin, on March 4, 1864. His mother died when he was an infant, and an aunt raised him as her own.

As a youth, Bloedel was much involved in athletics, and at one time he held records in nationwide bicycle competitions, as did his future friend J.J. Donovan. As a businessman, even while young, Bloedel gave bicycle-riding lessons and sold bicycle wheels. He attended the University of Michigan in Ann Arbor, graduating in 1885. Already a successful entrepreneur, he dealt in real estate while he was in college; this endeavor helped him finance his education. Little did he know then that acquiring real estate would be part of his phenomenal success in the future.

The boom of the West attracted Julius to Tacoma, Washington, in 1889. His travels took him farther north to Fairhaven in September that year, and he surmised that the railroad business was likely to make the Fairhaven area successful. There he met J.J. Donovan. After returning to Wisconsin to prepare for a move west, Bloedel came to Fairhaven permanently in March 1890.

In Bellingham, Bloedel began his employment with J.F. Wardner, the principal owner of the Samish Lake Lumber and Mill Company. It was Bloedel's first connection to the lumber industry. Following Wardner's example, Bloedel became involved in banking early in his life. He was instrumental in founding the Fairhaven National Bank. The *Fairhaven Herald*, in 1891, described him as "no deadhead in any enterprise in which he enlists."

Not many months after Wardner hired him, Bloedel invested in a business that would become the Blue Canyon Coal Mining Company, located at the southeast end of Lake Whatcom. Bloedel filed a mining claim in the area, recorded on April 1, 1891, for 160 acres. Part of this area would eventually become the town of Blue Canyon. Claims by Clarence W. Carter and Aaron F. Rice would later be added to the Blue Canyon conglomerate under the Lake Whatcom Coal Company. The Blue Canyon Mine was off and running. Bloedel in late 1891 was not rich, but he invested most of his assets in the Blue Canyon Mine. In July 1891, Wardner sold his interest in the mine to a group of men called the Montana Syndicate, most of whom lived near Helena, Montana, including Peter Larson, a railroad magnate and miner. Formally organizing later, the Blue Canyon Coal Company was officially begun on December 23, 1891, with Wardner, Bloedel, Donovan and C.W. Carter as its officers. Donovan became chief engineer. The Blue Canyon Coal Mine proved to be successful, at least at the start. The coal seemed to be good quality, it was abundant and the demand for coal on the West Coast was rising.

The same year, 1891, revealed that the terminus for the Great Northern Railway would be in Everett, not Fairhaven. The speculative excitement about the future of the Fairhaven area being tied to railroading was dashed. Businessmen in the area had to redirect their ventures or see their fortunes disappear. For a time, coal mining seemed to be a good investment, and it competed with lumbering to be the dominant industry around Lake Whatcom.

Integral to the coal mining industry was the transportation of the product to its buyers. Some investors, including J.F. McNaught of Anacortes, preferred connecting coal mining to the coast via Wickersham and Anacortes on a proposed Northern Pacific route, but Bloedel and Donovan chose Bellingham Bay. Bellingham was fifteen miles from Blue Canyon, while Anacortes was twenty-six miles distant. Blue Canyon required a connection to Bellingham, so these men formed the Bellingham Bay and Eastern Railroad to transport the coal to the harbor and coal bunkers at Whatcom. However, as the mine operations became troublesome due to fires, explosions and poor coal output, the three men turned their attention to timber. They would soon begin buying all the timberland they could acquire. Slowly, the Montana Syndicate members—except Larson—divested themselves of their investments in the area, and Bloedel, Donovan and Larson acquired the entirety of the businesses, both the coal mining and the lumber interests.

Bloedel married Mina Louise Prentice, a teacher from Saginaw, Michigan, in Fairhaven on October 20, 1898, and they moved to Seattle in 1911, though he maintained that it was for business reasons and not because his love of the Bellingham area had diminished. They had three children: Harris Prentice Bloedel (born 1900), Lawrence Hotchkiss Bloedel (born 1902) and Charlotte Van Alstyne Bloedel Brechemin (born 1905). The Bloedels, like the Donovans, were quite wealthy. The first Bloedel home at 1020 North Garden Street, in the Sehome neighborhood, built in 1900, would eventually become a site on the National Register of Historic Places.

Bloedel, Donovan and Larson gradually acquired the logging rights to the extensive forests around Lake Whatcom, as well as elsewhere, and they formed the Lake Whatcom Logging Company on August 11, 1898. Bloedel, Donovan and Larson had quite different backgrounds, but they were complementary. Bloedel was manager of a logging company and a coal mine. Larson was a railroad contractor. Donovan was a civil engineer. Each anted up $2,000 for twenty shares in the new lumber company. Larson was technically the president of the company, Donovan was vice president and Bloedel was operations manager and secretary. Larson, at the time, was far richer than the other two younger men. Larson told them to call on him if more money was needed. He would offer any financing they might need during hard times. Larson was more of a silent partner and source of investment capital for the trio. Donovan remained the builder and logistics person; he was well-liked and enhanced the company image as he interacted with the community and promoted the company's business ventures. Bloedel was the businessman who negotiated all the contracts and managed the financial affairs for the trio's multiple endeavors. The business would change its name to the Larson Lumber Company in 1901. Lumbering began at the southern end of Lake Whatcom near South Bay and moved northward. By 1904, these men owned twenty-two thousand acres of timber around Lake Whatcom. In a few short years, at the peak of the Bloedel-Donovan-Larson lumber empire heyday, they owned the rights to the timber of most of the two townships surrounding Lake Whatcom.

By 1911, Bloedel had begun to expand his timber empire into British Columbia. In 1913, Bloedel and Donovan purchased the Bellingham Bay Lumber Company (also called the Cornwall Mill), further enlarging their lumber dynasty. They named the conglomerate the Bloedel-Donovan Lumber Mills, which included the Larson Lumber Company, the Lake Whatcom Logging Company and the Cargo Mill on what is now Cornwall Avenue (then called Dock Street). Bloedel and Donovan further expanded the scope of their operation from logging and milling lumber to the production of wooden boxes, door sashes and other products. During

Julius H. Bloedel, circa 1925. *Whatcom Museum, 1980.0074.000162.*

its heyday, the Bloedel-Donovan enterprise, with Bloedel the president and Donovan the vice-president, operated "four sawmills, four shingle mills, a box factory, a sash and door factory, and one hundred miles of logging railway, with twelve locomotives, three hundred and fifty cars and necessary logging equipment," as described in Lottie Roeder Roth's *History of Whatcom County*. It employed an average of two thousand persons. It was worth $6.5 million.

The Great Depression hit the Bloedel-Donovan enterprise as it hit everyone else. Its financial strength began to dwindle, and in 1932, it defaulted on a loan for the first time in its history. Thereafter, the company struggled. It took out a loan in 1933 from the Reconstruction Finance Corporation under the National Recovery Act. By 1944, the company was in trouble again, and it began to divest itself of assets. It slowly disassembled the large lumber mill on Lake Whatcom.

Bloedel died on September 21, 1957, at the age of ninety-three. His wife, Mina, had preceded him in death in 1951. Prior to his death in 1946, he had donated approximately twelve acres of his holdings to the city of Bellingham to create Bloedel-Donovan Park, and it was dedicated to the city on August 11, 1948, the fifty-year anniversary of the founding of the company.

Bloedel was described as a devoted citizen of Bellingham who stuck with the town during bad financial times. Filled with great energy and business acumen, he offered wise counsel to many. Lottie Roth described him as personally being both "unassuming" and "kindly."

Bloedel was buried at the Evergreen-Washelli Memorial Park in Seattle.

PETER LARSON

Peter Larson was born on the island of Fyen (Fyn), Denmark, on July 11, 1849. His family was poor, and as a youth, Larson tended cattle and crops on the farm, often working long days to help support the family. He immigrated to the United States, arriving penniless in New York on May 19, 1871, at age twenty-one. Initially, he worked constructing the jetties at the mouth of the Mississippi River; later, after about two years, when he had repaid the company that bought him his ticket to New Orleans and saved a few hundred dollars, he went to Arkansas, where he began to learn the railroad business.

Larson then went north, where he spent some time in Minnesota and, later, in North Dakota. By 1879, the Northern Pacific was expanding toward

Peter Larson. *Whatcom Museum, 1996.0010.001025.*

Washington Territory, and Larson took advantage of the need for subcontractors. He first worked as a freight hauler and went on to build tunnels and lay tracks. He soon developed business and negotiating skills.

Larson was married in 1880 to Margaret Moran of Bismark, North Dakota. They had one adopted child, Mabel Agnes Lamey Larson, his wife's niece from Iowa. When in the Bellingham area, the Larsons lived at "Wardner's Castle," 1103 Fifteenth Street at Knox Street, purchased from J.F. Wardner only one year after the Wardners completed building it on South Hill. However, Larson's love was Helena, Montana, and he never considered Bellingham his real home. He also spent a great deal of time in Spokane with his businesses, keeping a suite of rooms year-round in the Ridpath Hotel in Spokane.

Larson would soon become rich through his success mining lead, silver and zinc. He started learning about lumbering when he needed timbers for his mines. He acquired a sawmill to produce these mining essentials, and he never looked back.

Larson joined with Bloedel and Donovan in 1898 to form the Lake Whatcom Logging Company. He began with a small investment of $2,000 but ultimately poured over $500,000 into this business, buying timberland around Lake Whatcom and elsewhere. Furthermore, as the railroading expanded in the Whatcom area, Larson put large sums of money into the Bellingham Bay and British Columbia Railway. He even invested in beer, breweries and flour.

Peter Larson died in Helena, Montana, on July 12, 1907, at the age of fifty-eight. His death certificate gave the cause of his death to be "liver cancer" that had been present for the preceding nineteen months. He allegedly contracted his illness when he was shipwrecked in frigid waters between Seattle and Victoria, British Columbia, on August 1, 1904, and forced to remain in the cold water for many hours. After his ordeal nearly drowning and dying of hypothermia, he was never the same vigorous and active man. This near-drowning and hypothermic experience profoundly affected his spiritual life, and his pastor would relate in his eulogy that it was his "Saul on his way to Damascus" experience. After touching the fringes of death and seeing men, women and children around him dying, Larson joined the Catholic Church.

Larson was considered one of the two richest men in the Northwest, being worth $10–25 million at the time of his death. The *Helena Independent* published his obituary on July 19, 1907, and included a eulogy by Catholic bishop John P. Carroll, who called him a "railroad contractor, miner, lumber king and captain of industry." Furthermore, "His clear mind, sound judgment, marvelous powers of observation, keen insight, broad grasp of situations, promptness of action compelled the admiration of his fellows, and, like the fabled alchemy, turned everything he touched into gold." Larson was rarely, if ever, accused of trampling others to achieve riches. Indeed, friends said that "his art was justice." Coworkers declared that he made every dollar he earned honestly. Additionally, he was generous, humble and frequently described as a fair boss who had a warm heart. Acquaintances did not identify him as a philanthropist; his generosity was more often quiet and anonymous, helping men with whom he worked as they had needs.

The *Helena Independent* reported that close friends knew Larson as "a man of few words and of a retiring disposition." His quietude could be interpreted as a distant personality, lacking in affection, but those close to him knew otherwise. He was devoted to his wife and adopted daughter and to his grandchildren. According to the *Missoulian* (July 13, 1907), "Mr. Larson is not a good mixer. He was always business from first to last and had no time or inclination to devote to social amusements. He had his close friends, and to them he was a whole-souled, genial host." Earlier, in 1902, the *Missoulian* said of him, "The ordinary recreations of humanity are a bore to a man whose only amusement is work....His social instincts, however, are not very marked, and although he belongs to the Spokane club and the Amateur Athletic club here, it is almost never that he is seen in either place." Nevertheless, his workers admired him for his honesty and his willingness to right any perceived wrongs between management and employees.

Larson, who had started out penniless in the United States at age twenty-one, became a millionaire from mining and railroad investments and from lumbering and banking. He gave the bulk of his estate to his wife, but he also gave philanthropically.

Larson was buried in the Resurrection Cemetery in Helena, Montana.

Edward Fitzherbert Gwavas Carlyon

Edward Carlyon was born to British parents on November 8, 1861, in New Zealand. He received his grammar school education in Canterbury, New Zealand, where he lived on the family ranch of thirty-three thousand acres. He thereafter went to Christ College and finished his degree studies at Cambridge University in England. After passing the bar and becoming a lawyer, he moved to Vancouver, British Columbia, where he observed that friends dealing in real estate were far more successful financially than lawyers. He decided to join the land speculation frenzy, and he moved to Whatcom in the fall of 1888.

With Reginald Jones, also a lawyer who had graduated from Cambridge University, Carlyon formed the firm of Jones and Carlyon in Sehome. Jones had a background in the railroad business as counsel to the Canadian Pacific Railroad Company and the Bank of British Columbia before he came to Whatcom County. Dealing in insurance and real estate, Jones and Carlyon occupied an office at the corner of Elk (now State) Street and Holly Street. Advertising themselves in both Bellingham newspapers and directories of the era as "real live, energetic and thoroughly reliable businessmen in every sense of the term," they concluded with the statement, "Their offices are without doubt the finest on the Bay, their list of properties large, and their patrons get fair and square dealing."

Carlyon soon purchased a three-hundred-acre tract of land at the north end of Lake Whatcom—an area later to be named Silver Beach—and he arranged for a road and a telephone line to be built to the area. Carlyon and Jones then established a syndicate that planned a community in the region, and they had the area platted for a town with a dock on the lake and a hotel strategically placed on the land sloping toward Lake Whatcom above the dock.

In addition to his land speculation, Carlyon was a cattle breeder, a skill learned from his father on the family farm in New Zealand. His Carlyon Gardens, a nearby farm, began in 1900 as the centerpiece of his cattle business. In his later years, he lived on Deemer Avenue, off the Guide Meridian, near the Van Wyck region of Whatcom County.

Carlyon married Lucille DuVall of Arkansas on August 3, 1904, in Seattle; they had one child, Helen Ada Lucille Carlyon, born on June 16, 1905. Lucille died on December 1, 1905. Carlyon remarried on November 15, 1919, to Isabella Thallon Hogg of Scotland. Her education made her far more sophisticated than the average Whatcom County resident; she spoke four languages and was a teacher, tutor and accomplished horticulturist.

Edward Carlyon died in Bellingham on September 25, 1939.

THE JENKINS FAMILY

The Jenkins family was prominent in Bellingham and in the development of the land around Lake Whatcom, especially the town of Geneva. Brothers Will, George and Leslie were instrumental in promoting the resources in the area.

William D. "Will" Jenkins was a politician and newspaperman. Born in Pekin, Illinois, on April 21, 1852, Will Jenkins grew up in Nebraska and Kansas. After working as a compositor in a printing office, he went on to become an editor and publisher.

Will Jenkins moved to Whatcom in 1885 and founded and published the newspaper *Whatcom Reveille* (which would later be called the *Bellingham Morning Herald* and, subsequently, the *Bellingham Herald*). He was the first mayor of the consolidated towns of Whatcom and Sehome, then called New Whatcom, where he served a total of three terms. Married three times and widowed twice, he had five brothers and three sisters. His first

Captain George A. Jenkins. *Whatcom Museum, 1996.0010.001458.*

wife, Elvira Axton Jenkins (they married on July 22, 1875), was his partner in the development of the Geneva region. They had three children: David C. Jenkins, Will D. Jenkins Jr. and Lulu Jenkins. Elvira died on January 25, 1890. On October 27, 1891, Will married Mary E. Hosmer, who died on January 25, 1899; he married Emma J. Rayl on May 1, 1900.

Will Jenkins fancied himself a farmer as well, calling himself a breeder and dealer in cattle, ponies and hogs. He ran the census bureau for the area of Western Washington in 1890 under President Harrison. Originally a Republican, he switched parties in 1892 to become a Populist. He then became editor of the newspaper *Champion* in 1892. He was elected secretary of state in 1896 and served from 1897 to 1901, being defeated for reelection in 1900.

George A. Jenkins (most often called Captain Jenkins) was born on August 9, 1864, in Nebraska. He was also married three times and widowed twice: he married Mamie B. Lysle Jenkins on March 25, 1891, Mary Shearon Jenkins on July 13, 1897, and Alan M. Royal Jenkins on June 27, 1917. In 1890, George Jenkins was manager of the Bellingham Bay Steam Ferry Line, located at the corner of Dock and Holly Streets. His major claim to fame was captaining steamboats on Lake Whatcom. He died on November 15, 1945.

Leslie A. Jenkins was born on October 9, 1866. He married Anna M. Jenkins on May 15, 1927. Early in his career in the Bellingham area (1888), he was the proprietor of the Whatcom and Geneva Stage Line. In 1890, he was the purser for the steamship *Mikado*.

David C. Jenkins (son of Will Jenkins) would become the "proprietor" of the Geneva townsite as it was developing.

Will Jenkins, George Jenkins, David C. Jenkins, M.E. Jenkins and M.B. Jenkins formed a corporation called the Bellingham Bay Syndicate.

Chapter 6

RAILROADS

In the late 1800s, railroads were the darlings of economic advancement. Businessmen in virtually all cities wanted the rails to come through their towns. Rail transportation was the ticket to financial growth, much as highways would be during the expansion of automobile traffic, as airline hubs would be to flight travel and as shipping would be to port cities. Businessmen saw the lure of having a transcontinental railroad pass through their town or—better yet—having it terminate at their coast. Such was the case for the Fairhaven, Bellingham, Sehome and Whatcom complex. Many financiers believed that coastal Whatcom County was destined to receive goods from across the country and would be the sending port to overseas markets. Bellingham would compete vigorously for the western terminus of the transcontinental railroad system. In fact, two railroad lines would consider using Bellingham as their access to the sea: the Great Northern and the Northern Pacific.

Progress was slow, however. The depression of 1873 retarded railroad development for nearly a decade. By about 1882, however, rumors had renewed the possibility of having a transcontinental line terminate in what would become Bellingham. Building construction was stimulated, and land speculation began afresh. The 1880s saw a resurgence of railroad development toward the West.

Eugene Canfield, once a state senator in Illinois, came to Whatcom County in 1883, and he began projects that would develop Bellingham Bay as a railroad destination. First, he founded the Bellingham Bay Railway and Navigation Company (BBR&NC) in 1883, with himself as president. This venture was projected to connect Bellingham to the Canadian Pacific Railway, where it was to terminate at Port Moody, British Columbia, slightly southeast of current-day Vancouver. There it would have access to the sea through the Burrard Inlet. Canfield's BBR&NC never succeeded in laying any track, however. It would be ended by Canfield joining with the New Westminster and Southern Railroad in 1888, which likewise was intended to join British Columbia with Bellingham, first passing through Blaine. This connection of Bellingham with Blaine to the north and with Sedro and Woolley to the south (it would become Sedro-Woolley in 1898) was to be the start of a system from British Columbia to Portland, Oregon.

Nelson Bennett, another powerful railroad magnate, founded the Fairhaven and Southern (F&S) Railroad in December 1888, intending to connect Bellingham to Canada. Construction began in 1889, with J.J. Donovan as the chief engineer. The route was completed in 1891; it would be a vital link in the Great Northern system.

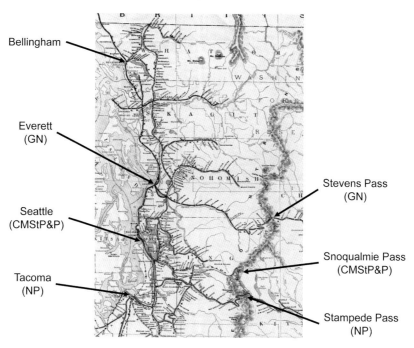

Map of rail lines from 1908. (GN: Great Northern; CMStP&P: Chicago, Milwaukee, St. Paul and Pacific; NP: Northern Pacific). *"Railroad Commission Map of Washington: 1910 Commissioners, H.A. Fairchild, John C. Lawrence, Jesse S. Jones,"* Manuscripts, Archives, and Special Collections, #WSU363, Washington State University.

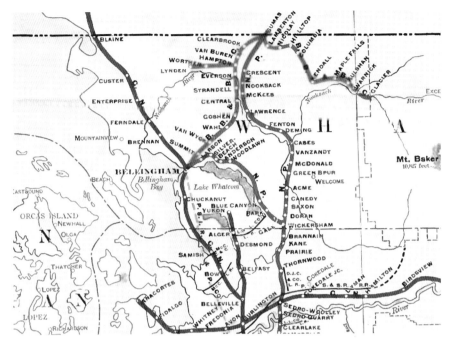

Detail from previous figure. *"Railroad Commission Map of Washington: 1910 Commissioners, H.A. Fairchild, John C. Lawrence, Jesse S. Jones," Manuscripts, Archives, and Special Collections, #WSU363, Washington State University.*

Another of the three major railroad projects (headed by Canfield, Cornwall and Bennett) was the Bellingham Bay and British Columbia (BB&BC) Railroad. Also begun in 1883 by Pierre B. Cornwall, the BB&BC sought to connect to the Canadian railway system. It began laying rails in June 1884. The BB&BC brought the first two steam locomotives to Bellingham in the fall of 1888, beginning operation on October 11, 1888. It would succeed in joining the Canadian Pacific at Sumas in 1891.

James J. Hill was the president of the Great Northern Railroad and, in 1891, was the prime decision-maker to site the terminus of the Great Northern Railroad in Everett. This choice dashed the hopes of many in the Bellingham area for an economic boom. Then the depression of 1893 engulfed the region. Hopes were shattered for economic salvation from a transcontinental railroad terminus. The Northern Pacific, the other major system that developers and speculators hoped would choose Bellingham as its major hub, chose Tacoma via Stampede Pass as its western terminus.

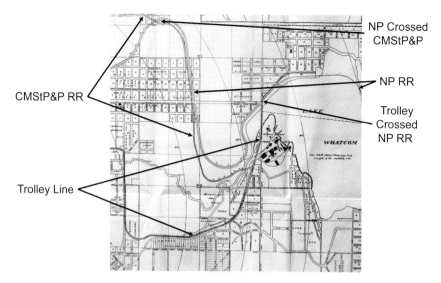

The railway system in Bellingham in 1922. The Northern Pacific was the first to complete a line to the Silver Beach area. The two lines—Northern Pacific and Chicago, Milwaukee, St. Paul and Pacific—crossed and both then progressed in parallel fashion (two railways) to the Bloedel-Donovan (formerly Larson) Lumber Mill and Silver Beach. The trolley crossed the Northern Pacific at Alabama Street, then coursed parallel to, and north of, the Northern Pacific. *Biery Papers, Commercial Map of Washington, Map #5-10, CPNWS.*

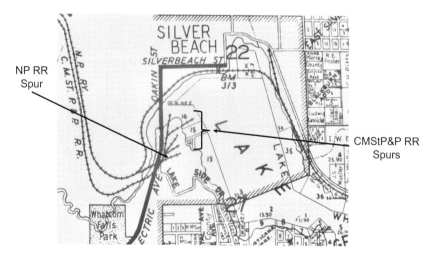

Details of railroad spurs from the Northern Pacific (NP) and the Chicago, Milwaukee, St. Paul and Pacific (CMStP&P) Railroads around Bloedel-Donovan Lumber Mills. The NP (formerly the Bellingham Bay and Eastern Railroad) had a single spur to the mills, while the main line went to Silver Beach and then to the east side of Lake Whatcom to Blue Canyon. The CMStP&P briefly merged with the trolley line, then issued four spurs to the mills and docks. *Adapted from Kroll Maps, Whatcom County, 1940.*

RAILROAD LINES IN THE EARLY 1900s

ROUTE	RAILROAD	COMMENTS
Major Routes in Whatcom and Skagit Counties		
Bellingham, Larson, Silver Beach, Agate Bay, Towanda (Sunnyside), Idlewild, Blue Canyon, Park, Mirror Lake, **Wickersham**	Bellingham Bay and Eastern, later absorbed by the Northern Pacific	
Bellingham, Larson, **Silver Beach**	Fairhaven and New Whatcom Electric Railway	Electric trolley
First proposed as **Bellingham** to **Sumas**, later developed as **Bellingham** to **Blaine**	Bellingham Bay Railroad and Navigation Company; route was actually completed by the Fairhaven and Southern and later acquired by the Great Northern	On paper only; construction was never started by BBR&NC
Bellingham, Squalicum Junction, Van Wyck, Noon, Wahl, Goshen, Central, Strandell, Everson, Hampton, Van Buren, Clearbrook, **Sumas**	Bellingham Bay & British Columbia, later becoming the Chicago, Milwaukee, St. Paul and Pacific	Spurs from the CMStP&P went to the Bloedel-Donovan Lumber Mill, built after the BB&E/NP line to Bloedel-Donovan Lumber Mill and Blue Canyon/Wickersham
Sumas, Nicolay, Hilltop, Columbia, Balfour, Kendall, Maple Falls, Warnick, **Glacier**	Bellingham Bay & British Columbia Railway, later absorbed by the Chicago, Milwaukee, St. Paul and Pacific*	

Route	Railroad	Comments
Bellingham, Marietta, Brennan, **Blaine**	Great Northern	
Bellingham, South Bellingham, Happy Valley, Hibridge, Grandview, Chuckanut, Samish, Edison, Sunset, Field, Roray, Maiben, Burlington, **Mount Vernon**	Pacific Northwest Traction Company (Interurban)	Electric trolley
Bellingham, Samish, Blanchard, Bow, Belleville, Mount Vernon, Fir, Stanwood, Marysville, Everett, **Seattle**, **Tacoma**	Great Northern	
Sumas, Wickersham, Sedro, Wooley, Arlington, Snohomish, Woodinville, Kirkland, Renton, Kent, Auburn, **Tacoma**	Seattle, Lake Shore and Eastern, later absorbed by the Northern Pacific	
Bellingham, Alger, **Sedro**, **Wooley**	Fairhaven and Southern, later absorbed by the Great Northern	
Anacortes, Sedro, **Hamilton**	Seattle and Northern Railroad, later acquired by the Great Northern	
Major East–West Routes		
Spokane, Ellensburg, **Tacoma**	Northern Pacific	Through the Cascade Range via the Stampede Pass Tunnel, still in use

ROUTE	RAILROAD	COMMENTS
Spokane, Ellensburg, **Everett** and **Spokane**, Ellensburg, **Seattle**	Chicago, Milwaukee, St. Paul and Pacific	Through the Cascade Range via Snoqualmie Pass Tunnel (Hyak to Rockdale), now inactive
Spokane, Wenatchee, Monroe, Snohomish, **Everett**	Great Northern	Through the Cascade Range via the Cascade Tunnel at Stevens Pass, still in use
Trans-Canadian Intercontinental	The Canadian Northern and Canadian Pacific were major east–west routes in Canada	Connected to U.S. railways at Sumas (Northern Pacific and Chicago, Milwaukee and St. Paul and Pacific) and at Vancouver, B.C. (Great Northern)

* The Chicago, Milwaukee and St. Paul became the Chicago, Milwaukee, St. Paul and Pacific. It was later simply called the Milwaukee Line.

Other railroads acquired by the Great Northern include the New Westminster and Southern Railroad and the Seattle and Montana Railroad.

Another railroad acquired by the Northern Pacific was the Seattle and West Coast Railway.

Many other smaller railroads were acquired by the larger systems.

Sedro (1884) and Woolley (1890) initially were separate towns, before merger into Sedro-Woolley (1898).

Bold = terminus.

The original railroad line from Blue Canyon Coal Mine to the Silver Beach area was owned by the Bellingham Bay and Eastern Railway (BB&ER). The Blue Canyon Coal Mine, the town of Blue Canyon and the BB&ER were inextricably intertwined, and the principal officers of these corporations overlapped. The BB&ER had been incorporated on December 17, 1891, and there were ten major investors, including Bloedel, Donovan and Larson.

The other investors were members of the Montana Syndicate and New York financiers. The original goal of this company was limited: to connect Bellingham to Wickersham by rail. From Wickersham, other rail lines could be accessed to extend the reach of the delivery of the Blue Canyon coal both north and south. The plan would change to connecting Bellingham to Blue Canyon around Lake Whatcom.

The BB&ER received its franchise for construction of a route from New Whatcom to Blue Canyon on December 18, 1891, just one day after its incorporation. The distance to be traveled on this railroad was only about twelve miles. It was indeed to be a tiny railroad. The officers of the BB&ER were Edward Eldridge, president; S.T. Hauser, vice-president; J.J. Donovan, secretary and treasurer and chief engineer; and Edmund Cosgrove and Peter Larson, directors.

Extensive contracts were let for portions of the railroad system needed for successful functioning: five hundred feet of Bellingham Bay waterfront property for coal bunkers and shipping wharves, terminals at Lake Whatcom, grading, laying track, coal cars and flatcars, logging cars, locomotives, rails and stationary engines.

A two-year contract was also negotiated with the Fairhaven and New Whatcom Street Railway to use its existing tracks for a portion of the route from Bellingham Bay to Lake Whatcom. In addition, the BB&ER negotiated an agreement with the BB&BC Railway to house its engine in the BB&BC enginehouse in Bellingham. The BB&ER would ultimately cost about $160,000.

Competition for the rail connection between Blue Canyon and Bellingham Bay was intense. The Seattle, Lake Shore and Eastern (SLS&E) announced on April 6, 1891, that it had completed the survey for connecting Wickersham to Blue Canyon. Its report declared that the Fairhaven and Southern Railroad would be part of the connection and that Fairhaven was to be the terminus. The BB&ER thus would compete with the SLS&E for the delivery of Blue Canyon coal. However, the SLS&E never succeeded in connecting to the Blue Canyon Coal Mine.

The BB&ER had been incorporated on December 17, 1891, though on November 7, 1891, the Blue Canyon Coal Company had already ordered a fifty-ton locomotive to be used on this hypothetical route, again highlighting the interconnection of these many business ventures. Construction of the wharf for coal transfer at Silver Beach on Lake Whatcom began simultaneously.

The development of the coal transportation system advanced piecemeal. During 1891 and 1892, the Blue Canyon Coal Company built and used a tiny spur from the northwestern shore of Lake Whatcom to connect to the street trolley system on Electric Avenue. Prior to the completion of the BB&ER around the lake, and beginning in 1891, the coal was hauled from Blue Canyon in small four-wheeled railcars on barges to the wharf at the site of the future Larson Lumber Mill at the northwestern end of Lake Whatcom. The coal cars would be delivered from the barges onto that short railway spur (about six hundred to seven hundred feet) that connected with the trolley car system at Electric Avenue. From there, the coal cars would use the portion of the Bellingham trolley line that went along Lakeway, Woburn and Kentucky Streets. After reaching downtown, the trolley rails connected to tracks on what was then called Pig Alley (later Puget Lane, between Elk Street and Railroad Avenue), making the final few hundred yards to the coal bunker at the bay on coal company rails. The citizens of New Whatcom themselves even contributed some funds to construct the final approach to the bunker, believing that any augmentation of downtown business would be advantageous to everyone.

DEVELOPMENT OF COAL AND TIMBER TRANSPORTATION SYSTEMS AT LAKE WHATCOM

YEAR	COMMODITY	SYSTEM
1891	Coal	Sacks or piles of coal on a barge to Silver Beach; wagon to Bellingham
1891	Coal	Rail car on barge to Silver Beach, coal company spur to Electric Avenue, trolley line (Lakeway, Woburn and Kentucky Streets) to Bellingham, coal company line to Sehome wharf
1892	Coal	Coal: Rail car on barge to Silver Beach, coal company spur to Electric Avenue, trolley line to Bellingham, coal company line to Blue Canyon wharf (the Blue Canyon Wharf replaced the Sehome Wharf)
	Timber	Timber: Log booms towed to Silver Beach by steam tugs, timber loaded onto rail cars on coal company spur to Electric Avenue, trolley line to Bellingham (wood processing plants)

YEAR	COMMODITY	SYSTEM
1892	Coal	Coal: Rail car on barge to Silver Beach, coal company spur to Electric Avenue, trolley line to Bellingham, BB&ER line to Blue Canyon wharf
	Timber	Timber: Log booms towed to Silver Beach by steam tugs, timber loaded onto rail cars on coal company spur to Electric Avenue, trolley line to Bellingham (wood processing plants)
1892	Coal	Coal: Rail car on BB&ER line to Silver Beach, then connecting to trolley line on Electric Avenue; BB&ER line in Bellingham to Blue Canyon Wharf in Bellingham Bay
	Timber	Timber: Log booms towed to Silver Beach by steam tugs, timber loaded onto rail cars on coal company spur to Electric Avenue, trolley line to Bellingham (wood processing plants), some timber to wood processing plants in the harbor and then to ships in the harbor.
1900	Coal, timber, lumber*	Rail car on BB&ER line to Silver Beach (some timber by log boom), then west and north around to Bellingham to downtown BB&ER line in Bellingham to Blue Canyon Wharf and ships
1901	Coal, timber, lumber*	Rail car on BB&ER line to Silver Beach (some timber by log boom), then west and north around to Bellingham to downtown BB&ER line in Bellingham to Blue Canyon Wharf and ships; Bloedel-Donovan began shipping lumber, as well as timber
1902	Coal, timber, lumber*	Rail car on Northern Pacific line to Silver Beach (some timber by log boom), then west and north to Bellingham to downtown Northern Pacific line in Bellingham to Blue Canyon Wharf, used for both coal and timber (Northern Pacific had purchased BB&ER)

YEAR	COMMODITY	SYSTEM
1913	Coal, lumber*	Rail car on Northern Pacific line west and north to Bellingham to downtown Northern Pacific line in Bellingham to Blue Canyon wharf (coal) and to ships (lumber). Most timber was processed into lumber by the Bloedel-Donovan Lumber Mills.

* "Timber" refers to unprocessed logs. "Lumber" refers to processed logs and includes shingles.

Bloedel-Donovan would eventually have timber processing plants both at Silver Beach and in Bellingham Bay.

"Bellingham" connotes the entire Whatcom/Sehome/Bellingham/Fairhaven complex.

It was clear, however, that the trolleys and the coal cars could not continue to use the same rails forever. If nothing else, there was a safety issue that needed to be addressed. Locomotives and heavy coal cars needed their own rails. No serious accidents occurred in 1891, but the need for separate rails demanded the completion of the BB&ER. The owners of the BB&ER even had dreams of connecting the line from Blue Canyon to Wickersham, where the Northern Pacific ran north to Sumas and south to Seattle.

At about the same time, the BB&ER contracted with Fairhaven Foundry and Machine Company for about $12,000 to make ten coal cars modeled on the Northern Pacific's design. Each car was to weigh about six tons, and each could carry ten tons of coal. Furthermore, the railroad contracted for the construction of a barge to ply the waters of Lake Whatcom carrying these coal cars. The barge was initially designed to carry twenty-one of these coal cars, but the final model was actually able to haul twenty-four. The turnaround time for these contracts was amazingly aggressive: the contract for the barge was let in March, and its construction at Geneva was to be completed by June 1. Construction of the many elements of the BB&ER was proceeding at lightning pace.

Furthermore, some political issues developed as, in May 1892, the laying of track began for the railroad line to the coal bunker on Bellingham Bay. Newspapers called it the "crossing war" between the BB&ER and the Great Northern, the disputed site being at about Polk and Tyler Streets, just west of Elk. Donovan's plan was to have the BB&ER cross above the Great Northern tracks on a trestle with forty feet of clearance, which

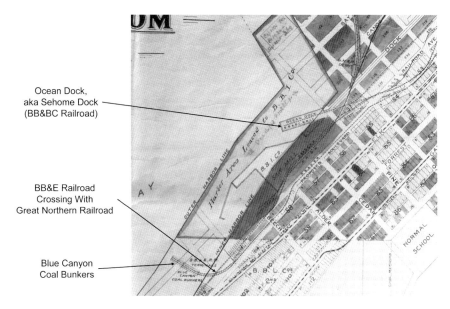

Ocean Dock, aka Sehome Dock (BB&BC Railroad)

BB&E Railroad Crossing With Great Northern Railroad

Blue Canyon Coal Bunkers

Crossing of the Great Northern Railroad with the Bellingham Bay and Eastern (BB&E) Railroad. BB&BC: Bellingham Bay and British Columbia. *"Map of the Town of New Whatcom, Whatcom County, Washington Territory,"* I. A. LaFavre, 1883, Bellingham Bay Improvement Company Records, Map #9-4, CPNWS.

Donovan thought was sufficient for all contingencies. The Great Northern executives disagreed and opposed the construction of the overpass. After a confrontation among hundreds of workers from both sides, restraining orders and court proceedings, the two parties reached an agreement, and the overpass was completed quickly.

Construction was also continuing rapidly at the Silver Beach end of the project. The first load of coal from Blue Canyon delivered by the BB&ER arrived on June 3, 1892, though it was actually taken to the Sehome wharf because the Blue Canyon coal wharf on the bay had not yet been completed.

The BB&ER officially opened on June 8, 1892, the day the first load of coal was transported from Blue Canyon to the bay by train. (The actual formal christening of the system was performed on June 30.) The railroad would eventually be called a Little Giant. Small in size, it would be large in its influence on Bellingham's economy.

The BB&ER was immediately successful, and it stimulated further coal and lumber traffic from Lake Whatcom, in addition to augmented passenger and cargo traffic. In the fall of 1892, the BB&ER built the one-hundred-passenger, eighty-ton, eighty-horsepower steamer *Ella* to work on Lake Whatcom. The *Ella* further increased the capacity of the BB&ER's system:

it could pull two barges that contained coal or tow log booms of lumber destined for elsewhere. Increased transport capacity stimulated a boom in other businesses; soon, on Lake Whatcom, there was a lumber mill, the Blue Canyon coal mine, two shingle mills and five logging camps, as well as three other potential coal mines under development.

The entire BB&ER line from Bellingham Bay to Silver Beach was not completed until January 10, 1902. At its peak, the BB&ER had two trains going from Fairhaven to Silver Beach and two from Silver Beach to Fairhaven (daily except Sunday). Eventually, one of these would go all the way to Wickersham. The trip with stops between Silver Beach and Fairhaven took between 50 and 140 minutes; the trip with stops between Fairhaven and Wickersham took 170 minutes.

The tiny railroad remained under the operation of the BB&ER for only a very short time. On October 8, 1902, the Northern Pacific bought the BB&ER for $500,000. The Northern Pacific took full control only two days later, on October 10.

Maintenance was always a financial burden for railroads. After the Northern Pacific acquired the BB&ER, the officers discovered that, even though the railroad was very young, many sections of the line already needed repairs. The original construction had used many trestles and small bridges as the line hugged the north and east edges of Lake Whatcom. While this design enabled a cheaper and more rapid completion of the route to Blue Canyon, frequent rockslides and erosion were already taking their toll on the integrity of the line. The Northern Pacific immediately began shifting the rails slightly

The railroad across the north end of Lake Whatcom started as the Bellingham Bay & Eastern Railroad, became the Northern Pacific and later was the Great Northern. This view looks toward the south. The Silver Beach Hotel was located to the right, just out of the frame. *Whatcom Museum, 1996.0010.003555.*

inland, eliminating many of the trestles and bridges as the rails were moved toward solid ground. By 1904, the track was much more stable. Eventually, the Northern Pacific merged with the Burlington and the Great Northern, and in April 1970, all were consolidated into the Burlington Northern system.

The BB&ER/Northern Pacific Railway coursed along the western edge of what is now called Scudder Pond, joining Electric Avenue where it now becomes Northshore Drive, at the intersection of what is today Alabama Street. The Northern Pacific hugged the shoreline to the end of Silver Beach, where the Silver Beach Hotel and White City were located. The railway then crossed the northern end of Lake Whatcom on a trestle bridge to reach the east side of the lake near where North Avenue currently joins the lake at Northshore Drive. The railroad line spanning from Silver Beach to the northeastern side of Lake Whatcom remained in place until at least 1950; maps show this railroad intact until at least 1954.

Small logging companies arose around Lake Whatcom's shores, and even more coal mines were established. With an estimated 500 million to 1 billion feet of timber alone to be harvested, the BB&ER was sure to have business at

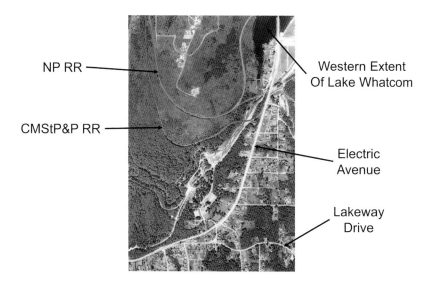

Aerial photo of Whatcom Falls Park from 1950. The two railroad lines can be seen as *U*-shaped paths through the woods in the upper half of this photo. The Northern Pacific (NP) is the uppermost line, beginning at the top left of this photo. It gives off a feeder line to the Bloedel-Donovan Lumber Mills (*upper right*) and then skirts the western side of Scudder Pond. The Northern Pacific spur line bridge over Whatcom Creek was located just feet to the south of where the current footbridge crosses Whatcom Creek, and just south of the dam. CMStP&P RR: Chicago, Milwaukee, St. Paul and Pacific Railroad. *Aerial Imagery Viewer, City of Bellingham.*

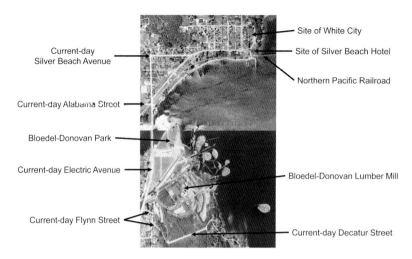

Composite aerial view of Silver Beach in 1950. At this time, the Bloedel-Donovan Lumber Mill was in the process of being dismantled. The remnants of the old lumber mill are at the lower left corner of the photo; the Northern Pacific Railroad passes along the extreme southern border of Silver Beach, where houses now sit, then across Lake Whatcom to the east side of the lake. The electric trolley would have followed approximately the path of the street, now called Northshore Drive, coursing slightly north of the railroad line. *Aerial Imagery Viewer, City of Bellingham.*

hand. The coal bunkers in the Bellingham harbor were developed to handle the coal, but timber could also be delivered at the same bunkers. Timber could then be processed at any of many mills around Bellingham Bay. As the timber/logging business expanded around Lake Whatcom, small mills constructed many feeder railroad spurs around Lake Whatcom to bring the logs to the main railroad line that hugged the edge of Lake Whatcom. The entire system was capable of handling one hundred thousand feet of timber daily and thousands of tons of coal.

The Chicago, Milwaukee, St. Paul and Pacific was built slightly later and took a slightly more southern route to Electric Avenue, passing on the east side of Scudder Pond and then briefly north along Electric Avenue. The Bellingham trolley system coursed along Electric Avenue to the Silver Beach Hotel. It was a few yards to the north of the Northern Pacific Railway after crossing over at Alabama Street, the trolley line and the Northern Pacific being parallel after the Alabama/Electric intersection.

Building of roads lagged behind both boat and train service to communities around Lake Whatcom. A road between Park and South Bay, hardly over three miles, was not completed until 1919; more complete road service around the south end of the lake was not available until 1930.

Remnants of the Chicago, Milwaukee, St. Paul and Pacific trestle in Whatcom Falls Park. It was built in 1915–16, and the last train used it in about 1959. The trestle was said to have been abandoned in 1963. Demolition occurred in September 2023. *Author's photo.*

Remnants of the Chicago, Milwaukee, St. Paul and Pacific trestle near Barkley Village, along what is now the Railroad Trail. Here, the CMStP&P crossed over the Northern Pacific on its way toward the Larson Lumber Mill (Bloedel-Donovan). It was also built in 1916. *Author's photo.*

Chapter 7

BELLINGHAM'S TROLLEY CONNECTION TO LAKE WHATCOM

To call itself a major city, a metropolis needed many amenities: sewers, lights, electricity, water, sometimes gas (frequently used for lighting), entertainment centers, police and fire departments, streets that functioned in all weather conditions and transportation hubs. Between 1880 and 1890, transportation centers usually involved trolley systems. No self-respecting major town in the United States was without its trolley system, and such a conveyance established the town as modern. Bellingham was indeed modern.

The initial separation and subsequent mergers of Whatcom, Sehome, Bellingham and Fairhaven presented difficulties for the development of the trolley line. First, the town of New Whatcom started its own trolley system, the Bellingham Bay Electric Street Railway, founded on July 17, 1890. This trolley system, which connected New Whatcom and Sehome, opened on March 29, 1891, soon after the two towns consolidated on February 16, 1891. (Fairhaven and Bellingham had also joined each other in May 1890.) Looking ahead, the owners negotiated with Whatcom County to build an extension of the trolley out to Lake Whatcom. The trolley company required that the town of Silver Beach give 15 percent of the town's land for its tracks to seal the deal. Fairhaven, on the other hand, was unwilling to grant the Bellingham Bay Electric Street Railway permission to build within its city limits. The development of a trolley line to Lake Whatcom was stimulated by the founding of yet another business, the Lake Whatcom Electric Railway Company. Its goal was to beat the Bellingham Bay Electric Street Railway in its own plans to extend its line to Lake Whatcom.

Fairhaven had its own trolley line (the Fairhaven Electric Railway Company) that also began operating in 1891. The two systems, Fairhaven's and New Whatcom's, engendered stiff competition, and though the two lines ended close to each other near the border of Fairhaven, the companies refused to connect them. Financial difficulties forced the Fairhaven Electric Railway Company to go bankrupt, but it was quickly replaced by the Fairhaven Street Railway. Even then, connecting the two systems was impossible because of the competition and jealousy between the two towns. Passengers had to walk about one block from the end of one to the beginning of the other, often through the muddy streets, or they could travel by wagon between the two. By February 1892, passengers had complained enough: the two companies acquiesced and joined lines at a common point, also merging commercially as one company.

On February 3, 1892, the Fairhaven Street Railway acquired the tracks and equipment from the Lake Whatcom Electric Railway in return for the Lake Whatcom Electric Railway owners' acquisition of shares of ownership in the Fairhaven company. The competition between cities extended into the merger itself, as each line wanted its name to appear first in the new name of the merged company (New Whatcom and Fairhaven, or Fairhaven and New Whatcom). They had to resort to a coin toss to determine which name appeared first. Fairhaven won the toss, so the name of the new company was the Fairhaven and New Whatcom Railway. The Whatcom residents, poor losers, persisted in referring to the new trolley company as the New Whatcom Railway. The first trip to Lake Whatcom occurred on February 18, 1892, a scant few days after the merger. Newspapers reported that nearly three thousand citizens made the trip on that day on the new "Lake Line" (the population of the entire city then was only about nine thousand).

To travel to Lake Whatcom, the electric railway took passengers from the intersection of Dock and Holly Streets to Silver Beach, a distance of about six miles. It took twenty-three minutes, and the fare was ten cents one way. The route followed today's Bellingham streets of Kentucky, Woburn, Lakeway and Electric. (Of course, Electric Avenue is so named because it carried the electric trolley to the terminus of the line at Silver Beach.) The trolley facilitated both the emergence of Silver Beach as a community and the construction of the Silver Beach Hotel, soon to be followed by the White City Amusement Park. An amusement park was another requirement for a city in the 1890s to be considered modern.

E.F.G. Carlyon, the man responsible for building the Silver Beach Hotel, improved the primitive road from the Bellingham area to Silver Beach

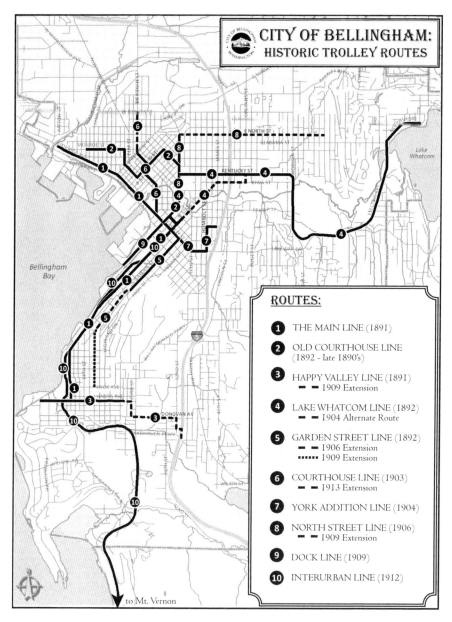

Trolley lines. *Whatcom Museum, Historic Trolley Routes—Newell and Jewell, 2015, City of Bellingham.*

(roughly the equivalent of Alabama Street today), and he instituted a horse-drawn stage system to service the region in 1890. The Whatcom Lake Stage Line left the Pioneer Stables at eight o'clock in the morning, returning at five o'clock in the afternoon. Losing the stage business to the

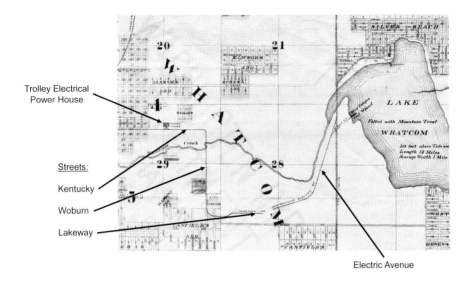

Lake Whatcom Trolley Line, Fairhaven and New Whatcom Electric Railway, 1893. The Bellingham Bay and Eastern Railroad had a short spur from the Blue Canyon Coal Wharf to the Fairhaven and New Whatcom Electric Railway for movement of the coal cars. The trolley line coursed along what today is Kentucky Street, Woburn Street, Lakeway and Electric Avenue to Northshore Drive. *Bellingham Bay Improvement Company Records, Map #8-1, CPNWS.*

trolley was hardly a tragedy because the new trolley had a much larger passenger capacity and it was far more rapid. Carlyon had envisioned a grand hotel, as well as an entertainment venue for Lake Whatcom, and the trolley was going to make it happen.

In 1891, Bellingham had less than 3 miles of trolley track; by 1905, Bellingham's trolley system had been expanded to 16.25 miles of rails.

By the end of 1905, Stone and Webster, Incorporated (Charles A. Stone and Edwin S. Webster), a Boston-based company, had purchased and was operating the Bellingham trolley system. The company added four new trolleys to the Lake Whatcom Line, and it built turnouts on the line to accommodate the multiple cars traversing the route from downtown Bellingham to Lake Whatcom at Silver Beach. Continual upgrading of the trolley system was necessary because the streets in Bellingham were being changed from wooden planks to asphalt, requiring changes in the tracks and the crossties used.

Bellingham residents loved the new unified system. The cost had decreased to a mere five cents to ride anywhere the system functioned. Activity at Lake Whatcom was intense. The Silver Beach Hotel had opened on April 1,

One car of the Fairhaven and New Whatcom Electric Railway that served Silver Beach. Note the sign advertising the balloon ascension and band concert at White City. *Whatcom Museum, 2001.0012.000007.*

The Fairhaven and New Whatcom Electric Railway served Silver Beach, circa 1912. *Buswell Papers, #515, CPNWS.*

1892, and the newly merged trolley company constructed a pavilion and grandstand at the Silver Beach end of the line.

The Fairhaven and New Whatcom trolley system would eventually collapse into bankruptcy, despite the fact that, in some years, it had over fifty thousand passengers. Its two-employee cars remained simple but elegant. However, other modes of transportation appeared. Motor coaches became more common. These vehicles were faster and often more direct than the fixed-route trolleys. Jitneys, touring cars and auto-stages caught the favor of travelers, and the trolleys soon had serious competition. On November 30, 1938, the trolley carried its last passenger.

Chapter 8

BOATS ON LAKE WHATCOM

To the observer today, the image of working boats on Lake Whatcom is an anachronism. Now we see many small private fishing boats and powered pleasure craft, the uncommon sailboat, an occasional Jet Ski and frequent kayaks and rowboats.

In 1860, seven prospectors made what might have been the first recorded boat trip by non–Native Americans on Lake Whatcom. Headed to the South Fork of the Nooksack River to scout prospective mining sites, they took a crude trail from Bellingham Bay to Lake Whatcom. On August 24, 1860, they built a small raft and crossed the lake to approximately where Sunnyside would later be located. From there, they bushwhacked eastward over the hills, where they found little of value for mining.

In the late 1800s, rowing from Silver Beach to Blue Canyon or Park under the best of circumstances took about four hours; men tried sailboats, but generally, the winds were not reliable for sailing on this lake. Therefore, more dependable and rapid means of transportation were needed, but to envision tugs pulling logs to the lumber mill, barges filled with coal and passenger ferries for hire sounded like a different world. And it was.

The Lake Whatcom Steamboat and Transportation Company was formed on September 26, 1884, to develop Lake Whatcom routes, but it never achieved success. On May 22, 1885, Michael Anderson built a two-ton "yacht" for use on Lake Whatcom. Some descriptions called it a sloop, and it was named the *Bell-Lena* (or *Belle-Lena*). However, it was powered by a sail, and the winds on Lake Whatcom proved to be too light and unpredictable for it to be useful as a commercial venture.

In the early years, the boats plying Lake Whatcom were constructed and initially put into service elsewhere, then transported to Lake Whatcom by various means. Some were pulled to the lake by horses or yoke cattle. Later, others would be hauled to Lake Whatcom on the backs of railroad flatcars.

Understanding the evolution of boat traffic on Lake Whatcom is difficult. Not only did ships have many names over the course of their existence, but they were also frequently repaired, rebuilt, combined with parts from other ships and reoutfitted as needs changed. Boats were lengthened and shortened; passenger cabins were enclosed; passenger cabins were opened. Owners came and went, and a new owner usually meant a new paint job and a new name. The *Edith* is a prime example of such an evolution. Over the course of decades, she underwent changes of structure, appearance and name at least seven times. Furthermore, not infrequently, a boat would be cannibalized, with portions of her machinery removed and reinstalled on different boats, while the structure itself had a different fate. Traditionally, the name of a ship follows the hull. Many variations in names would be seen over the years.

Boats on Lake Whatcom*

Hull	Names	First Service on Lake Whatcom	Sank, Burned or Changed Name
Geneva	*Geneva*	1888	1893
Rose	*Rose*	1890	1894
	Emma D	1894	?
Edith or *Edith R*	*Edith*	1890	1890
	Inger[1]	1890	1890
	Mike Anderson	1891	1892
	Mike Anderson-2[2]	1893	Circa 1901
	Cora Blake	Circa 1901	Circa 1903?
	Vesta	Circa 1903	?
	Dodo	?	?
	Brud (a.k.a. *Brudd* or *Bried*)	?	Circa 1906

Hull	Names	First Service on Lake Whatcom	Sank, Burned or Changed Name
	Cora Blake	Circa 1906	1914
Regie	Regie	1891	1903
Shamrock[3]	Shamrock	1892	?
White Swan	White Swan	?	1902
Little Edith	Little Edith	?	Circa 1914
	Emma D	1894	?
Thistle	Thistle	1892	1901
	Adelaide	1901	1910
Elsinore	Elsinore	1903	Circa 1919
Ella	Ella	1892	1906
	Prentice	1906	1914
	Charlotte	1914	1957; 1966
Marguerite	Marguerite	1905	1924
Ramona	Ramona	1907	?
Aurora Borealis	Aurora Borealis	1908	?
Geneva No. 2[4]	Geneva No. 2	1909	?
Comet	Comet	1910	1924

Dates are approximate.
*After Galen Biery, CPNWS.
[1] Contemporary newspapers all spelled this ship "Inger," but Mike Anderson's child, after whom the boat was christened, was listed as "Ingar" in census records. The census in 1885 listed "Ingar" as a ten-year-old female child of Mike Anderson; the 1889 census listed the child "Ingar" as a fifteen-year-old boy.
[2] The Mike Anderson-2 used the hull of the Mike Anderson, but the inclusive dates for her service are uncertain.
[3] The Shamrock incorporated the engine and boilers from the Mike Anderson.
[4] Interestingly, Jenkins did not refer to this boat as the Geneva-2 or the Geneva-II but simply as the Geneva, even though there had been a previous Geneva.

Boats in Service on Lake Whatcom*

Year	Boats in Service
1890	*Geneva, Edith, Inger*
1891	*Mike Anderson, Rose, Geneva*
1892	*Regie, Rose, Thistle, Shamrock, Geneva, Mike Anderson*
1893	*Rose, Ella, Regie, Geneva, Thistle, Shamrock*
1894	*Emma D, Thistle, Ella*
1895	*Thistle, Regie*
1896	*Thistle, Regie*
1897	
1898	*Emma D, Thistle, Regie, Ella*
1899–1901	
1902	*Regie, Adelaide*
1903	*Elsinore*
1904	*Elsinore, Adelaide, Cora Blake*
1905	*Adelaide, Cora Blake, Elsinore*
1906**	*Adelaide, Marguerite*
1907	*Ramona, Elsinore, Marguerite*
1908	*Adelaide, Elsinore, Marguerite, Ramona*
1909	*Adelaide, Elsinore, Ramona, Geneva #2, Marguerite*
1910**	*Comet, Marguerite, Prentice, Ramona, Geneva #2*
1911	*Comet, Elsinore, Marguerite, Prentice, Ramona, Geneva #2*
1912**	*Comet, Marguerite, Prentice, Geneva #2, Ramona*
1913	*Comet, Elsinore, Marguerite, Prentice, Geneva #2, Ramona*
1914	*Charlotte, Comet, Elsinore, Marguerite, Geneva #2, Ramona*
1915	*Charlotte, Comet, Elsinore, Marguerite, Geneva #2, Ramona*
1916	*Charlotte, Comet, Elsinore, Marguerite, Geneva #2*
1917	*Charlotte, Comet, Marguerite, Elsinore*

YEAR	BOATS IN SERVICE
1918	*Charlotte, Comet, Marguerite*
1919	*Marguerite*

*After Galen Biery, CPNWS.

Boats listed are those found in newspapers from that year. Others may have been in service, as well.

** There is no mention of the *Elsinore* in newspapers from 1906, 1910 and 1912, though she may have been in service then, too.

THE *GENEVA*

The *Geneva* was brought from Seattle as the first steamboat to work Lake Whatcom, though she was not built on Lake Whatcom. Sharing a name with the town Geneva that Will D. Jenkins founded, she was owned by Jenkins and Lee W. Marcy.

The *Geneva* was rather small at 8.44 tons and 38 feet long, with a 7.5-foot beam and a draw of 4 feet. Formerly called the *Albany*, she was constructed in 1885 at Albany, Oregon. With an 8-horsepower engine, she was able to achieve 8 to 10 miles per hour.

Bringing the *Geneva* to Lake Whatcom from Bellingham Bay in August 1888 was a monumental task. There were no good roads; there was no railway. The steamship was heavy and bulky. After disassembling her—separating the ship from the machinery—on August 19, the Jenkins brothers and Lee Marcy loaded the 8.44-ton steamboat on a wheeled carriage in Whatcom and pulled her over four miles with six oxen. The *Geneva* was then reassembled at Lake Whatcom.

Capable of holding twenty-five to forty passengers plus some freight and mail, the *Geneva* was initially commanded by George A. Jenkins. (Previously, George's brother Leslie Jenkins had delivered the mail in a rowboat.) The *Geneva*'s first trip was on August 28, 1888. She primarily ran between Geneva and the southern end of the lake, stopping at many points along the way.

By the summer of 1889, the *Geneva* was very busy, holding excursions by pulling a huge barge that included space for a musical band. She would be used for special group outings, especially on Sundays. The barge allegedly could hold up to three hundred passengers, though rarely were that many people on board. The fee was fifty cents for the round trip. By 1890, she was also servicing the Silver Beach area.

The *Geneva*, 1888. *Biery Papers, #3551, CPNWS.*

The *Geneva* was the workhorse of the lake in the early 1890s. She ran Monday, Tuesday, Thursday and Friday, leaving Silver Beach at eleven thirty in the morning; on Wednesday and Saturday, she left at nine thirty, and on Sunday, she ran from Silver Beach to Geneva every hour. Clearly, Sunday was the most popular day for picnics at Lake Whatcom.

On March 5, 1891, the *Geneva* was approaching the Silver Beach dock when ice broke through the stern hull. The captain beached the ship to prevent her from sinking. She was successfully repaired. However, on October 10, 1893, after she was tied to the Geneva dock in anticipation of a coming storm, a gale tore her loose, and she drifted onto rocks, where she wrecked. She was declared a total loss with an estimated value of $2,000.

THE *EDITH*

Edith was a common woman's name in the late 1800s and early 1900s, as well as a common ship's name, confounding the identification of steamers because so many ships had the name "*Edith*" in the Bellingham Bay and the Puget Sound regions.

There were at least four *Ediths* in the Puget Sound area (one of which, the *Edith E*, serviced Lake Washington, Seattle–Kirkland–Houghton–Yarrow), and at least two additional boats in the Bellingham area named *Edith*. The first *Edith* in Whatcom County began her life on the Nooksack River in about 1884. She was also known as the *Edith R* and would be the precursor to the *Cora Blake*. The second *Edith* was a small craft that operated on Lake Whatcom in about 1914–15, also called the *Little Edith*.

The *Edith*, or the *Edith R*, was a stern-wheeler eventually run on Lake Whatcom by Michael Anderson. She was also distinguished by being called the river steamer *Edith*. This *Edith* had been built at Sehome (some reports say Whatcom or New Whatcom, but they were nearly synonymous) for about $3,000 in 1883. Captain Simon Peter Randolph was the owner and builder; the ship was named after Randolph's daughter Edith. (Some reports had her machinery coming from a boat called the *Comet*, though this could not have been the same *Comet* as the one built in 1910.) As a stern-wheeler with the rudder behind the wheel, she was 77.27 tons and 75 feet long (some sources say 65 feet), with a 16-foot beam. (In addition to frequent reconstructions and name changes, the reported size of any given steamboat varied greatly, depending on the source of the report. The *Edith* was also said to weigh 58 tons.) She was taken south and put into service on the White River (a tributary to the Puyallup River) in 1884. That same year, Robert Emmett Hawley, J.L. Hann and D.P. Quinn bought her from Randolph for $2,000. They deployed her to use as a passenger and freight boat on the Nooksack River from 1884 to 1889, serving mostly from Bellingham Bay to Hawley's Landing in Lynden (slightly west of the site where today's Hannegan Road crosses over the Nooksack, just on the southeast edge of Lynden). The stern-wheeler's first trip up the Nooksack occurred in February 1884, and local Native Americans called her the *hias canim*, or "big canoe."

Today, it seems unrealistic that a stern-wheeler could navigate the Nooksack, but it was a somewhat different river then. Logjams were constant threats. For years, a particularly large logjam—an accumulation of tons of logs, debris, branches and sticks—blocked the Nooksack River. A community effort to clear the river began in September 1876, and by February 1877, the Nooksack was navigable as far as Lynden and slightly beyond. The first steamboat began working the Nooksack River in 1878, reaching as far as Hawley's Landing at Lynden. Smaller steamboats were able to travel as far upstream as Deming. Soon, there were four ships that served the Nooksack River: the *Advance*, 66.97 tons; the *Triumph*, 107.39 tons; the *Nooksack*, 133.32 tons; and the *Edith R.*, either 77.27 or 58 tons, depending on which source one believes. This route, however, had its challenges. In the dry season, the river could be too shallow, and during the rainy season, a steamer might encounter rapids, large floating tree trunks or new logjams. In good weather, the round trip from Bellingham Bay to Lynden could take three days. The *Edith*—as well as the other vessels—would accept just about any freight, charging $5.50 per ton for the Bellingham Bay–Lynden run. (The course of the Nooksack would later change so that it emptied into Bellingham Bay instead of Lummi Bay.)

The *Edith* received a new hull in 1890, which changed her size to 60 feet long with a 14-foot beam (likely accounting for both the change in the length, from 75 to 60 feet, and the tonnage, from 77.27 to 58). The new *Edith* ran aground and wrecked on the mudflats near Lummi on May 9, 1890. The *Fairhaven Herald*, the Tacoma *Daily Ledger* and the Sehome *Morning Gazette* reported that a leak caused her to tip so far that she filled with water and sank, resulting in a "total wreck" with an extensive loss of cargo worth over $5,000 and damage to the boat worth $2,500. Other reports said that as she was going over a dangerous sandbar approaching the Nooksack River, a heavy squall or gale capsized her. The *Edith* was described as "going to the bottom," suggesting that she was not simply aground in shallow water. The local beach was strewn with cargo: beans, sashes, doors, etc. The *Edith* was taken to the Whatcom Iron Works on May 13 for repairs, and she was saved from being a total loss.

After initial repairs, the *Edith* took a few runs to Lynden, but she was then moved to service on Lake Whatcom, with plans to renovate her further there.

The *Edith*, when she was a river steamer, docked along the Nooksack River, circa 1883–84. Note the rear paddle wheel with the rudder behind her. *Whatcom Museum, 2014.0008.000212.*

Since she was such a large craft, many people believed it impossible for her to make such a long journey overland. Nevertheless, in June and July 1890, the company of Shewey and Jackson contracted to transport her to Lake Whatcom for $550. The renovation plan for the fall of 1890 at Lake Whatcom was to mimic the steamship *Mikado*, apparently the local standard of luxury.

The transport of the *Edith* from its location near Bellingham Bay to Lake Whatcom in 1890 was expected to take ten days, but it was far more difficult than anticipated to tow this large vessel to Lake Whatcom, taking almost fifty days. Her boiler and other heavy machinery were first removed to lighten her mass. She then was placed in a cradle-like structure to protect her integrity during the transfer. Thereafter, she was pulled on rollers (with huge timbers under her belly) up Thirteenth Street (now Holly), then on Elk (now State Street) and finally over the plank road on Alabama Hill that had been built by Carlyon and Jones to serve the Silver Beach Hotel. The mechanism used to move the ship involved many horses pulling on long lines to traverse the 3.5 miles and 316-foot elevation of Lake Whatcom above the bay, not counting the excess work to ascend and descend Alabama Hill itself. The many impediments to the move included encounters with bears that spooked both the horses and the workers. The procession was able to move only about two city blocks per day.

The move itself became a source of entertainment for residents around the bay. Newspapers reported almost daily on the *Edith*'s location. Crowds gathered daily to watch her progress—or lack thereof. Four teams of horses were used to move her, though a special apparatus was needed for raising her from the bay or for ascending abrupt grades. The journey became a

The *Edith*, at approximately Holly and Elk Streets, being towed on her way to Lake Whatcom. This is the only known photo of the *Edith* during transit to Lake Whatcom and is taken from a newspaper article. *"Who Remembers…"* Bellingham Herald Archives, *February 27, 1922, CPNWS.*

metaphor for progress impeded ("as slow as the *Edith*"). The *Edith*'s movement was chronicled in local papers from June 6 to July 25. During the trip, some citizens even suggested that tickets be sold for a Fourth of July spectacle: "Ride the *Edith* to Lake Whatcom."

To Carlyon and Jones's dismay, the weight of the ship damaged much of their plank "highway" from the bay to Silver Beach. The weight of the boat snapped many of the "stringers" on the road. The Sehome *Morning Gazette* termed her ascent up Alabama Street a voyage up the "long hill."

After arriving close to Lake Whatcom on July 11, 1890, the *Edith* presented even further problems. On July 15, she was still 250 yards from the shore. Even launching her into the lake proved difficult. Initially, the workers tried to pull her into the lake using the steamboat *Geneva*, the only other steamer working on Lake Whatcom at the time, with no success. Finally, on July 25, a combination of efforts was successful. Estimates placed the financial loss to the moving company at about $350; it had contracted for $550, but the total cost was over $900. The *Edith*'s first real voyage saw her travel between Silver Beach and Park on August 8, 1890, as she transported the mail that day. She was the first paddle wheeler on Lake Whatcom. She even had a race with the *Geneva*, but who won is not recorded. The *Edith* was the largest steamer ever to work on Lake Whatcom.

The *Edith* was very soon taken out of the water as planned and rebuilt with a new hull. Portions of the old hull were discarded near the Geneva Mill.

THE *INGER*

After her renovations, the *Edith* was rechristened the *Inger* on September 3, 1890, after Anderson's daughter. (All newspaper accounts record the name as *Inger*, though census records list Mike Anderson's child as "Ingar.") She plied the Silver Beach–Park run. But tragedy awaited. On September 26, 1890, the *Inger* burned while at the Park dock (the dock was owned by Michael Anderson), leaving only the *Geneva* again to service Lake Whatcom for a period of time. The *Inger*'s owners at the time of the fire were John Kilcup and Phil M. Isensee. The *Inger* fire also consumed the dock at Park, and nearby homes (including Anderson's) were barely saved by efforts of local firefighters. Burning to the waterline, the *Inger* sustained $2,000 in damages, and she was declared a total loss. She had no insurance. The fire apparently had started in the engine room, perhaps from rags used to wipe the machinery.

THE *MICHAEL "MIKE" ANDERSON*

The *Mike Anderson* was another one of the first boats on Lake Whatcom. She was to be built in the style of the "old *Mikado*." (The *Mikado*, after which the *Mike Anderson* was to be designed, was a steam-powered vessel used as a ferry between Fairhaven and New Whatcom, with stops in Bellingham and Sehome. She was described as long, narrow, fast and elegant.) The *Mike Anderson* was to be about sixty feet long. Michael Anderson purchased the remains of the *Inger* for his project in early October 1890 and planned to reoutfit her with new machinery. By mid-October 1890, Anderson was well on his way to repairing the ship. Unfortunately, on December 18, 1890, a tree fell on and damaged the *Inger* as she was being rebuilt, but construction resumed thereafter. The *Inger* received a new engine and boiler, and the hull was repaired by Bellingham Bay Iron Works. She was rechristened the *Mike Anderson*.

Completed around July 1891, the *Mike Anderson* was in service on Lake Whatcom at least by August 1891, resuming a Silver Beach–Park route. The new ship had an open upper deck, in contrast with the *Edith*, whose upper deck was enclosed. Not all had gone smoothly in her construction, however. Near the end of the process in July, Bellingham Bay Iron Works had to take Anderson to court to demand payment of $350 for work it had performed on the engine for the *Mike Anderson*.

The *Mike Anderson* was in service from 1891 to 1892. J.A. Roby purchased her on July 7, 1892, for $2,000. On Saturday–Sunday, October 8–9, 1892,

The *Cora Blake*, May 1, 1904. By this time, the *Cora Blake* may have been renamed the *Vesta*, but she was always commonly referred to as the *Cora Blake*. Note the rear paddle wheel. *Whatcom Museum 1996.0010.007107.*

the *Mike Anderson* sank at the Silver Beach dock during high winds and rain, as she foundered and tilted. Because the bilge tank doors were open, water filled the bilge, and the ship sank to the bottom of the lake. Within days, plans were made to raise her. The engine and boiler were salvaged on November 29, 1892, and they were placed in the stern-wheeler *Shamrock*. Apparently, only the machinery itself from the *Mike Anderson* was retrieved in 1892, because in 1893, newspapers reported that the hull was to be raised from the lakebed and converted into a barge after being underwater for nearly a year. The hull was finally raised and towed to Park, where reconstruction began on April 20, 1893. The *Mike Anderson* thus began a new life.

Ownership of the *Mike Anderson* changed frequently, and she was renamed the *Cora Blake* after receiving a new paint job, the hull blue and the pilothouse yellow. The name *Cora Blake* stuck through many owners, and the stern-wheeler worked Lake Whatcom under that name, mostly towing log booms and transporting shingle bolts.

THE *VESTA* AND THE *DODO*

Following the evolution of this hull, the *Cora Blake* thereafter tragically ran onto the rocks at Lanktree Point.* She was subsequently rebuilt in 1903 with a shortened hull, measuring 50 feet (the original *Edith* was 60–75 feet, depending on the date of the description), with a beam of 14 feet and a draft of 2.5 feet. She was later rechristened the *Vesta* (which was described as being 45–48 feet long, with a beam of 14–15 feet and a draft of 2.5 feet). The *Vesta* went into service in April 1903. After another brief stint with the name *Dodo*, she was purchased by the Larson Lumber Company on January 1, 1906.

THE *BRUD*

Many reports have this late iteration of the *Mike Anderson* being renamed the *Bried*, but more likely, this was a near-phonetic, but incorrect, spelling of *Brud* (also incorrectly spelled *Brudd*). This name was derived from Prentice Bloedel's nickname for his brother Lawrence Bloedel. Prentice called Lawrence "Brother," but in his early years, as a child, he could not pronounce "brother" and instead said "brudder"; this was shortened to "Brud."

---

* Otherwise spelled Langtree or Langtry.

In her waning years, the *Brud* was sold to the Geneva Mill, and she was again called the *Cora Blake*. She burned in 1914 near the Geneva Mill, between Strawberry Point and Geneva. Captain C.R. Hover was on board when the ship caught fire, and he brought her to the shore and tied her to the dock near the Geneva mill. Thereafter, he cut her free when it became obvious that the fire could not be contained. To protect the Geneva dock, the ship was pushed farther out into Lake Whatcom to prevent the fire from spreading, and she was finally towed and grounded near Strawberry Point, never to be rebuilt.

The *Shamrock*

The *Shamrock* had been under construction at Thomson's Mill by Roby and Johnson, and on Friday, December 9, 1892, she was towed to Silver Beach to receive the engine from the *Mike Anderson*. Her owners expected the *Shamrock* to be ready for service by January 1893, with Roby as captain.

The extent of the *Shamrock*'s use is unknown. She is rarely mentioned in descriptions of Lake Whatcom travel, though in 1918, one report said that there were five vessels in service: *Shamrock*, *Ella*, *Thistle*, *Regie* and *Rose*. The *Regie* and the *Thistle* were the fastest, while the *Shamrock* was the roomiest. She was described as a "lake stern wheel kicker" in the *Fairhaven Herald* on March 19, 1893. The *Shamrock* would later find new life as the *White Swan*.

The *Little Edith*

A second Lake Whatcom *Edith* was the *Little Edith*. She was used as a substitute craft for the Geneva Mill after the *Cora Blake* burned in 1914. The Geneva Mill rented and operated her; the owners were brothers Archie and Jesse McCullough. Charles Hoover was the captain.

Catastrophe awaited the *Little Edith*. Captain Hoover had been navigating on Lake Whatcom in the fog without a compass, and unable to see what was ahead of his ship, he recognized his peril. Declaring that he did not want to proceed further, Hoover encountered opposition. Mill superintendent (and, arguably, Hoover's boss) Bill Ferguson was on board, and he countermanded Hooper's judgment so that his merchandise could be delivered on time. Thereafter, the ship foundered on the rocks at Lanktree Point. Hooper disembarked, walked all the way to Silver Beach and resigned in disgust, leaving the *Little Edith* stranded on the beach.

The *Rose*, renamed
the *Emma D*,
date unknown.
*Whatcom Museum,
1996.0010.001434.*

The ship was dislodged and repaired, but another disaster lurked ahead. The final sinking of the *Little Edith* occurred near Watkins Point in about 1915, after she once again ran aground.

The *Rose* and the *Emma D*

The first steam vessel actually built on Lake Whatcom was the *Rose*. (The original *Geneva* was the first steamboat to work Lake Whatcom, but she was built elsewhere.) James H. Rosener was the builder, starting his project in 1887 but not completing it until December 1890. The *Rose* ran a passenger service from Park to Silver Beach, leaving Park at ten o'clock in the morning and Silver Beach at one thirty, stopping wherever necessary along the way.

The *Rose* was also designed to be able to tow barges filled with coal or coal cars from Blue Canyon to Silver Beach. Local newspapers described her as small, little, dainty, jaunty or trim.* The *Rose* was renamed the *Emma D* in 1894 by George W. Douglas, her new owner, in honor of his wife. The *Emma D* was sold again in January 1903, but her name remained the same.

Like so many boats of the era, the *Emma D* burned—at the Silver Beach area—and was a total loss.

---

* *Bellingham Blade*, June 7, 1898.

THE *ELLA*

The *Ella* was built by E.F. Lee of Seattle; construction took place at the Blue Canyon company's wharf (the Larson Mill) opposite Silver Beach near where Bloedel-Donovan Park is today. While the *Ella* herself was built at the Larson Mill, the engine was cannibalized from a ship assembled in Victoria, British Columbia, originally constructed in 1880. *Ella* was sixty-two feet long with a fourteen-foot beam, powered by a seventy-horsepower steam engine (at first, she burned coal; later, wood, requiring two cords per day; still later—after she had been converted to the *Charlotte*—oil). She was launched on November 19, 1892, and her major purpose was to haul coal from Blue Canyon.

The *Ella* was named after Ella Downs, wife of the superintendent of Blue Canyon Mine, M.E. Downs. The captain of the *Ella* was Henry Reasoner. When the railroad took over *Ella*'s task of bringing coal from Blue Canyon to Silver Beach, the *Ella* began towing log booms from the southern portion of Lake Whatcom to the northern extent of the lake, either to deliver them to the Bloedel-Donovan mills or to transport them by train to mills on the edge of Bellingham Bay. The *Ella* was able to tow 250,000 board feet of fir logs per trip.

While her major function was to tow log booms or coal, on May 30, 1893, the *Ella* began carrying passengers as well. In 1893, the round-trip fare for combined trolley tickets and boat tickets, New Whatcom–Silver Beach–Blue Canyon/Park and back, was seventy-five cents per person, and in her heyday, the *Ella* would make three trips per day between Silver Beach and Park. At the peak of activity on Lake Whatcom, there were four to seven boats working the Silver Beach–Blue Canyon route. The trip usually took about two hours, and the boat fare for one passenger was about fifty cents round trip. However, the *Ella* never competed in any meaningful way with these other passenger boats.

On February 6, 1893, the *Ella* became trapped in ice on Lake Whatcom but was not seriously damaged. She was partially remodeled in June 1900 for passenger use only.

In November 1900, a storm pounded the vessel against the piles of a wharf to which she was tied and tore a hole in her hull. She sank in fifteen feet of water, but she was reconstructed and continued to work as the *Ella*.

The *Ella*, 1901, at Blue Canyon, with coal chutes barely visible on the right. *Biery Papers, #0791.2, CPNWS.*

The *Ella*, with Captain George Jenkins sitting on the bow, circa 1900–10. *Biery Papers, #2675, CPNWS.*

The *Prentice*, 1890. *Biery Papers, #790, CPNWS.*

THE *PRENTICE*

The *Ella* was rebuilt in 1906, renamed the *Prentice*, after Prentice Bloedel, Julius Bloedel's son (Julius Bloedel's wife's maiden name was Prentice). The major job of the *Ella*, a.k.a. *Prentice*, was to tow large coal barges from the Blue Canyon Coal Mine to Silver Beach.

THE *CHARLOTTE*

In 1914, the *Prentice* was decommissioned, and her engine was moved to another vessel named the *Charlotte*, a boat that had been built in 1911 and continued to function for the next forty-three years. This *Charlotte* was sixty-one feet long, with a fifteen-foot beam and a nine-foot draw. The *Charlotte* was named after Bloedel's daughter (who dedicated her at the ship's christening). She towed log booms from various sites around Lake Whatcom to Silver Beach. After logging decreased around Lake Whatcom, the *Charlotte* was retired as a tug for log booms; her last trip was on November 24, 1957. She was sequentially sold to various buyers, but rotting of her wooden construction led to the *Charlotte* sinking near Strawberry Point.

The *Charlotte* sat in the water for about two years before local boating history enthusiasts decided to restore her to a useful function. In November 1959, the *Charlotte* again resumed activity on Lake Whatcom. One of her

The *Charlotte*, date unknown. *Whatcom Museum, 1996.0010.001444.*

major roles was the "Christmas Ship." Brightly decorated, she would tour the lake, stopping wherever groups of people congregated for Santa to hand out Christmas candy to children. In addition, during the summers, she was known as the Burger Boat, maneuvering from dock to dock, acting as a mobile fast-food carry-out restaurant.

The *Charlotte* sank at Wildwood Park at the south end of Lake Whatcom in January 1966 in a severe windstorm. She was raised successfully, but with extreme difficulty, on September 28, 1967, and she was towed to the area of the Geneva Mill, close to the hull of the *Cora Blake*, just off Lake Whatcom Boulevard. She never regained a useful function thereafter, and she sank again on Halloween 1975. An attempt to raise her in December 1975 resulted in her disintegration. However, years later, in 1993, her unique steeple engine was retrieved.

The *Ramona* and the *Geneva-2*

As technology progressed, the type of boat on Lake Whatcom changed. The naphtha launch was a faster, smaller version of a passenger conveyance compared to the older steam-powered vessels on Lake Whatcom, and various boats of this vintage emerged. George A. Jenkins developed two new boats of this type for Lake Whatcom, naming them the *Ramona* and the *Geneva* (a second-generation *Geneva*, not the early steamship that had been christened in 1888). His were actually powered by gasoline rather than naphtha. Construction was slated to begin in November 1906, and these two boats were built to carry fifty to sixty passengers each. Jenkins had envisioned the town of Geneva as a pleasure retreat with picnic areas, parks and connections to other recreational venues. Boating races and regattas were part of the Silver Beach Hotel/White City scene, as well as the general activity around Lake Whatcom.

THE *RAMONA*

The *Ramona* was a gasoline launch built in a large warehouse at the corner of Elk and Willow in Bellingham. When finished, she was transported to the lake on two flat railroad cars. Costing $4,000, she was fifty-five feet long with a nine-foot beam, powered by a three-cylinder, fifty-horsepower engine. Elegantly constructed, she had a hull of oak, spruce and fir. Her doors were oak. The *Ramona* was capable of a speed of eleven to twelve miles per hour, and her final configuration was said to hold about one hundred passengers (though other estimates of fifty were likely more accurate). Some reports called her a "floating palace." Her service was initiated in May 1907. Trips

The *Ramona. Buswell Papers, #858, CPNWS.*

between Silver Beach and Geneva (Strawberry Point) could be accessed every thirty to sixty minutes.

Admission to Jenkins's parks was free, and in 1907, round-trip transport on the *Ramona* from Silver Beach was $0.20. Ramona Park was the site of Ramona Camp, a YWCA retreat. This camp comprised four tents that were designed to give rest and relaxation to young women of the time, and the camp could accommodate ten girls at once, costing $3.50 per week (or $2.50 for those not sleeping in the camp). Very close to Geneva, this retreat cost only $0.50 for those spending just one night, and this fee included supper, breakfast and lodging. Meals alone were $0.25 each.

The *Ramona* made stops at Silver Beach, Geneva, Rusticana (a part of the town of Geneva), Ramona Park and Reveille Island, another of Jenkins's picnic sites. Jenkins's newspaper ads described Reveille Island as "the most beautiful island in the world."

The Second *Geneva*

The second ship named *Geneva* was forty feet long and had an eighteen-horsepower gasoline engine. She was launched in June 1909, and Jenkins later lengthened her by an additional fifteen feet and changed to a sixty-horsepower gasoline engine in March 1910.

The *Geneva-2*, circa 1900–20. This ship was quite similar to the *Ramona*. *Buswell Papers, #854, CPNWS.*

All Normal Students Should Avail Themselves of a Trip On Lake Whatcom

—o—

GET UP YOUR PICNICS AND EXCURSIONS

Charter one of the fine passenger boats

RAMONA OR GENEVA

And Have Your Own Private Party

A TRIP TO REVEILLE ISLAND, BLUE CANYON COAL MINE, THE TROUT HATCHERY, RAMONA PARK AND THE BIG LOGGING CAMP. ALL CAN BE VISITED IN ONE DAY.

ITS COSTS YOU BUT LITTLE   PRICES VERY REASONABLE

SUNDAY SCHEDULE—Every hour from 8:30 a. m. to 6:30 p. m.—Between Silver Beach, Geneva, Ramona Park and Manning's big Logging Camp. Camp in full operation on Sundays. Boats leave from Silver Beach Wharf at end of Lake Car line.   Fare 10c

PHONE MAIN 2712 OR SEE

GEO. A. JENKINS   414 High St.

Advertisement for excursions on Lake Whatcom, May 1913. "Normal Students" refers to Washington State Normal School at Bellingham, a teachers' college that would eventually become Western Washington University. *From the* Messenger, *May 1913, CPNWS.*

The *Ramona* and the *Geneva-2* were used mostly as passenger boats, though occasionally, they were used for towing. Jenkins improved the parks at Reveille Island, Ramona Park and Geneva Park, and he provided free admission to these sites to promote travel on his boats.

Geneva-2 was ultimately sold for use on Bellingham Bay and, yet later, moved to Lake Washington. Likewise, the *Ramona* was sold and moved south, where she was used on the Ballard–Kingston run.

THE *ELSINORE*

The *Elsinore* was another boat owned by George A. Jenkins. Originally built in New York in 1900 at a cost of $7,000, she was first used on Lake Washington in Seattle between Leschi and Madison Park. The boat was rather small, only five tons. She was sold for $10,000 and transferred to George A. Jenkins on

Lake Whatcom in April 1903, though the first reports of her service on Lake Whatcom were in October 1903. George A. Jenkins's brother Leslie A. Jenkins was the engineer. Described as "a trim little steamer," she could achieve a speed of fourteen knots with her fifty-six-horsepower engine.[*] With a length of fifty-five feet, a beam of ten feet and a depth (draw) of four feet, she was also called "palatial." This "floating palace" (a description that had also been given to the *Ramona*) had mahogany fittings, upholstered seating, electric lights and cherry woodwork, and her capacity was fifty to eighty passengers.

Jenkins marketed the ship as a pleasure craft, for passengers only, and at first, she was not used for hauling logs or coal. Jenkins was trying to develop his picnic sites around the lake. Toward the end of the *Elsinore*'s life, however, she was used to tow log booms, decidedly a step downward in stature.

On April 5, 1908, the *Elsinore* partially burned. She had been docked for the night at her boat landing, and investigators suspected that the fire originated in the engine room. She was towed into the lake to protect nearby buildings and the wharf from the fire. The damage was estimated to be worth $600. The *Elsinore*'s owners were able to repair her, however.

By 1909, an "automobile stage" was operating between Bellingham and the Geneva area (Rusticana, to be precise), decreasing the demand for boat traffic on Lake Whatcom. Bellingham residents could now be driven to the edge of the lake with no need to go first to Silver Beach. However, the *Elsinore* had been repaired by then, and she once again serviced the lake for those who preferred boat travel.

By 1911, the Lake Whatcom Steamboat Line, run by George A. Jenkins, dominated the service on Lake Whatcom, having the *Elsinore*, the *Marguerite* and the *Comet* as part of its fleet. A "rate war" broke out in June 1911, with Jenkins trying to corner all the business. He charged twenty-five cents for round-trip fare from Silver Beach to Park or Reveille Island, with further reduced rates for closer destinations along the route.

In 1913, the *Elsinore* suffered another mishap as she hit a chain connected to a log boom near Larson's Mill. The chain tore a hole in the hull, and in less than two minutes, the *Elsinore* sank in sixty feet of water. She was back in service soon, however, and ads in 1914 listed her as one of the active boats on the lake.

Yet another sinking was reported in 1915 during a gale on the lake near the Larson Mill, probably as floating logs smashed into the *Elsinore*'s hull. She had been relegated to towing logs by this time, and there was no

----
[*] *Bellingham Reveille*, May 5, 1903.

The *Elsinore*, 1903, with the Silver Beach Shingle Company in the background on the left. *Whatcom Museum, 1982.0043.000030.*

insurance on the boat. Nevertheless, she was back in service in 1916, and she continued through 1917.

In 1918, she was being beached on a skid to begin some repairs when some rotten wood on the hull was smashed, and she was never repaired. Eventually, the *Elsinore* met the same fate as so many other vessels on Lake Whatcom: she burned, near Lanktree Point.

THE *MARGUERITE*

The *Marguerite* began her life as the *Emma Florence* in Olympia in 1893. As a 29-ton steamer, she was 58 feet long with a 12.2-foot beam and a 3.4-foot draw. Capable of 13 miles per hour, she held 75 passengers. In 1898, she was rebuilt and became the *Marguerite*, serving the Olympia–Hartstene Island run until 1903; later, she served the Everett–Langley–Mukilteo and Everett–Snohomish routes before coming to Bellingham (on July 26, 1905) where she traveled back and forth from Bellingham to Anacortes and, on the weekends, between Bellingham and Lummi Island.

On December 2, 1905, the *Marguerite* appeared on Lake Whatcom after being transported there on a railroad flatcar; she began service on Lake Whatcom in 1906, where she plied the Silver Beach–Blue Canyon run.

The *Marguerite* was perhaps the best-known and best-loved of the passenger boats on Lake Whatcom. She carried regular passengers, as well as picnic groups, parties, barges with dancers, berry pickers and weekend revelers (often drunken loggers and miners who treated her with less than the respect she deserved).

A famous accident occurred on board the boat on January 26, 1907. Captain Hector Gawley caught some of his clothing on the rotating engine shaft, and it pulled him into the machinery, crushing the upper parts of his right arm, breaking some ribs, puncturing his lung and inflicting additional injuries to his head. A streetcar trolley took him to town, where he insisted on going to his home rather than to the hospital. He was later taken to the hospital, where doctors attended to his injuries. He survived, but with a permanent disability.

The *Marguerite* herself also encountered hard times, wrecking on February 9, 1907. That day, the fog was so thick that one could not see more than about three feet ahead. On a trip from Park to Silver Beach, the *Marguerite* ran aground on rocks at Lanktree Point, which tore a two-foot hole in the bow hull. The *Elsinore* was nearby and rescued the twenty passengers on board. Within two weeks, the *Marguerite* had been repaired successfully, but she had another encounter with rocks on April 18, 1908, though the damage was not as severe. Similarly, she grounded on September 16, 1917, but suffered no significant damage.

In 1919, the *Marguerite* was sold to the owners of the *Comet*, the only other passenger boat still in operation on the lake. (The automobile had begun to decrease the use of passenger boats around the lake.) While complete control of lake passenger traffic allowed the owners to maximize efficiency, they could see that the need for passenger boats was decreasing.

Moored at her dock near the Dakin Street bridge in Silver Beach on June 3, 1924, the *Marguerite* caught on fire, forcing bystanders to tow her into the lake to prevent other structures nearby from burning—a scenario that was all too common for boats on Lake Whatcom. She was quickly completely enveloped in flames, and the dock itself caught fire, too. The dock was mostly salvaged, but the boat was a total loss. The *Marguerite* sank near today's Bloedel-Donovan Park. There she lay for years, part of her hull visible as it projected above the waterline. She was finally removed in 1947, towed to the beach and burned, to make way for Bloedel-Donovan Park.

THE *THISTLE* AND THE *ADELAIDE*

The *Thistle* was constructed as the *Kate L. Wardner* at Port Townsend in 1889. Three different *Thistles* were constructed in the region during this era, one in

The *Marguerite*, circa 1910–20. *Whatcom Museum, 2010.0055.000168.*

1889, one in 1890 and one in 1892. At fourteen tons, the *Thistle* to be located on Lake Whatcom was forty-five feet long with a ten-foot beam.

George A. Jenkins and Frank M. Jenkins bought the *Thistle* and brought her to Lake Whatcom, transported on the Fairhaven and New Whatcom Electric Railway and the Bellingham Bay and Eastern Railway from the bay to the lake. She went into service on the lake in October 1892, one of five vessels the Jenkins family had brought to Lake Whatcom. The Jenkinses sold the *Thistle* to the Pittman family of Geneva on February 2, 1893.

Competition for paying passengers and dominance on Lake Whatcom was fierce. On July 30, 1895, the *Thistle* and the *Regie* held a race from Silver Beach to Woodlawn, with the *Thistle* as the winner.

The *Thistle*'s name was changed to the *Adelaide* in 1901 after it was sold to George Douglas. ("Adelaide" came from Beulah Adelaide Douglas, daughter of Captain George Douglas.) In September 1894, the ship was enveloped in fire near Woodlawn, and she burned to the waterline. The damage was worth $1,000. Although the ship's value was only $2,700, she was repaired and put back into service by October 1894.

In March 1904, the *Adelaide* was relegated to towing log booms. However, Douglas renovated the ship in April 1904 to make it more desirable for passengers.

By 1905, the round-trip fare from the north of the lake to the south was fifty cents. The *Adelaide* continued to service passengers through 1906–08.

Fares were adjusted for the purpose of trips on Lake Whatcom with berry pickers in the summer paying only half fare.

But tragedy struck, as it frequently did for many of the steamers on Lake Whatcom. The *Adelaide* burned beyond repair on February 8, 1910, while tied up at the wharf at Steeley's Landing between Lanktree Point and Woodlawn. The fire originated in the furnace of the engine, and the boat quickly burned to the water's edge. She was a total loss, valued at $1,500. The owners used the insurance money to build the *Comet*, a smaller boat that carried fewer passengers, and the engine from the *Adelaide* was removed to put into the *Comet*.

THE *REGIE*

The *Regie*, a small steam-powered vessel at 12.95 tons, was built in Chicago. Brought to Lake Whatcom on September 28, 1891, it belonged to James Thomas Brannian of Blue Canyon. The *Regie* burned four cords of wood per day as it ran the route between Park and Silver Beach twice daily. The *Regie* coordinated her connection at Park with the stage that ran from Park to Wickersham; riders could catch the train at Wickersham southbound to Seattle or northbound to Sumas and Canada.

The *Regie* was docked for repairs near Silver Beach on February 23, 1894, when a workman lit a fire on board so the pipes would not freeze, and the fire spread to the rest of the boat, causing about $1,000 in damage (the total

The *Thistle*, later renamed the *Adelaide*. *Biery Papers, #1655, CPNWS.*

The *Regie.*
Whatcom Museum,
2001.0072.000014.

value of the boat was estimated at $3,000). She was rebuilt and running again by March 1895.

The *Regie* again burned—this time beyond repair—at South Bay near Park on April 2, 1903. Only the engine and boiler were salvaged, and they were repurposed for use on land.

THE *AURORA BOREALIS*

The steamer *Aurora Borealis* was built in Tacoma and transported to Lake Whatcom, arriving on March 27, 1908. This vessel was owned by M.B. Christopher and was 27.5 feet long with a 6-foot beam. She could hold only 18 passengers and had a 10-horsepower engine, capable of speeds up to 10 miles per hour. Steering wheels were located front and back so the boat could be driven from either end. She cost $1,500 to build, and she was put into service in April 1908.

THE *COMET*

The *Comet* was launched in June 1910 as a passenger and freight vessel. She was built by Captain S.P. Randolph (who also built the *Triumph* and the *Edith R.*) near the Upright Shingle Mill on the north end of Lake Whatcom at a cost of $2,500. She was one of the few steamers built on Lake Whatcom itself, using the steam engine from the *Adelaide*, which had burned earlier in the year. Small at fifty feet long and eleven feet in beam, she was named after Halley's Comet, which had made an appearance in April 1910.

The *Comet* ran a route from Silver Beach to Geneva to the south end of the lake at Colonel Moore's Park.

The *Comet* grounded off Geneva on November 12, 1923, but she suffered little damage.

A near-disaster occurred on June 4, 1924, when the *Comet* was towing a scow loaded with students from the local normal school (later known as Western Washington University) to their eighty-acre camp (called Normalstad) at the south end of the lake. Between twenty-five and fifty students were being towed on the barge behind the *Comet* when many of them moved to one side of the scow to watch a swimmer, causing it to tilt. The scow partly filled with water, and some students went into the water, but it was only waist deep, and no serious injuries were reported. The next day, it was reported that the rope between the *Comet* and the scow had broken and the bow of the scow had tilted into the water. The *Comet* itself was not damaged.

The *Comet* finally wrecked on September 22, 1924. At the time, she was the only boat working Lake Whatcom. During a heavy gale near Hildebrand's Landing, logs broke loose from a nearby log boom—owned by the Bloedel-Donovan Mills—that had escaped its moorings near Park. The *Comet* was nearby, though securely tied, and the logs crushed her hull. After the storm, one of the logs was found resting on the *Comet*'s pilothouse. The *Comet* was finally towed to deep water and allowed to sink, somewhere between Reasoner's Point and Reveille Island.

Other Vessels

The *White Swan* was another stern-wheeler operated by Lee Pittman. She had been built from the remains of the *Shamrock*. She sank near Olsen Creek in 1902. The *Owl* was a smaller craft that had limited use on Lake Whatcom.

Lake Whatcom Motor Boat Club

The Lake Whatcom Motor Boat Club was formed in 1904 (some reports say 1909), though its activity waned as enthusiasm for the White City carnival at Silver Beach diminished. However, the club persists as the oldest motorboat club in the state. It was originally located at Watkins Point in Geneva. Yearly

Start of the fifty-mile Puget Sound Championship Power Boat Regatta, Lake Whatcom, July 25, 1912. The nearest boat is the *High Ball*. *Whatcom Museum, photo by J. W. Sandison, X.3219.006729.*

boat parades on the Fourth of July often attracted—and still attract—scores of boats of various styles, from antique reproductions to elegant sailboats to precise restorations.

Motorboat races were popular on Lake Whatcom in the early 1900s, climaxed by the Puget Sound Championship Speedboat Races in 1912. These races were testing grounds for new boat hulls and engines. The club underwent a resurrection of sorts in 1995.

LAKE WHATCOM MAIL SERVICE

The mail service around Lake Whatcom initially depended on boats, both small and large. Leslie Jenkins provided the first mail delivery around the lake in a small rowboat. Thereafter, as steam-powered vessels began working the lake carrying passengers, delivering cargo and towing timber and coal barges, the mail was carried on the *Geneva*, the *Shamrock* and the *Thistle*, to name a few. By 1902, the BB&E Railroad was delivering two pouches of mail, one for Blue Canyon and one for Wickersham (the final miles traveling by stagecoach). Rural Free Delivery began in 1906, at which time there were about 120–150 homes around Lake Whatcom with about one thousand total inhabitants. Henry Pederson was the mail carrier from 1906 to 1925, using his boat the *Roseau* (a private craft, not used for passengers).

Navigation Dangers on Lake Whatcom

People and homes were not immune from hazards on Lake Whatcom. Landslides occurred infrequently but could be devastating. Occasionally, heavy rains collapsed the hillsides above the lake, causing an avalanche of trees, mud, sticks and debris mostly down the east side of the lake. One such landslide occurred in November 1892, sweeping two people living in a cabin into the lake. They survived but were carried 150 yards into the lake before they were able to swim to shore. More recent floods, or "debris torrents," occurred in 1917, 1949, 1971 and 1983, particularly along the Smith Creek drainage basins. These events are frequently called floods because of the large volume of water involved. However, they are more accurately termed avalanches, landslides, debris torrents or debris flows because of the massive amount of trees, logs, branches, rocks, soil, sand, sediment and mud involved. The most recent occurred on January 10, 1983.

Chapter 9

COAL MINES

Coal Mines: An Overview

The Pacific Northwest spawned many lucrative businesses in the early years of its settlement by White men. Some would seem obvious: lumbering and all its affiliated industries, fishing and canning and even railroad development. However, today, the image of coal mining is not one that comes to the mind of most Northwesterners, especially those in Whatcom County.

Coal production was one of the first industries to visit the shores of Bellingham Bay. Most of the sites are obscure today: the Pattle Mine, the Sehome Mine, the Bellingham Mine. Even less recognizable are the mines that circled Lake Whatcom: Blue Canyon, Silver Beach, Glen Echo, Geneva, Rocky Ridge, South Bay, Dellesta, Woodlawn, Whatcom Creek and Manley were but a few of the claims touted as likely to bring riches to their investors. Unfortunately, most never produced coal ore at commercial quantities or quality, but the three mines in Bellingham would set the stage for coal mining fever to develop around Lake Whatcom.

Pattle Coal Mine

William Pattle was a British member of the Hudson's Bay Company who tried to develop a timber business venture on Lopez Island in 1852. Native Americans had told him about "black fire dirt" that they used for cooking

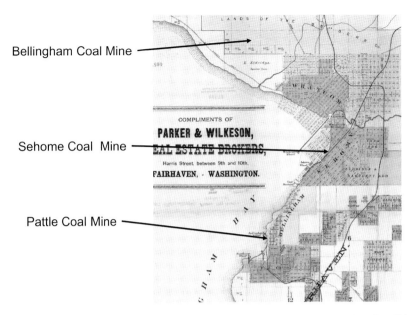

Coal mines around Bellingham Bay. *Adapted from Whitney's Map of the Bellingham Bay Cities and Environs, Whatcom County, Washington, 1890, Biery Papers, Map #4-3, CPNWS.*

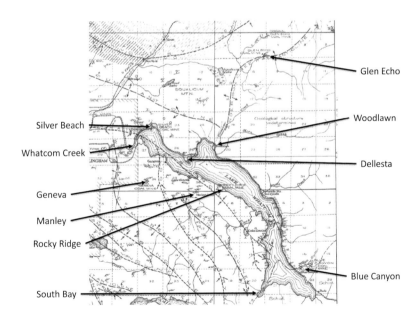

Coal mines around Lake Whatcom. *Adapted from Olaf P. Jenkins,* Geological Investigation of the Coal Fields of Western Whatcom County, Washington, *State of Washington Division of Geology, Bulletin No. 28, Olympia, WA, 1923.*

and heating. Their discovery was coal at the edge of Bellingham Bay near what today is the Taylor Dock leading up to the Chrysalis Inn, at Taylor and Tenth Streets. The location was once called Pattle Point, at the border between what would become Fairhaven and Bellingham. The opening to this coal mine was at the top of today's pier leading from the hotel and spa to the boardwalk below.

The coal was discovered in October 1852, and Pattle filed his claim in January 1853, but mining did not begin until later in 1853. The claim would ultimately yield only about 2,500 tons of coal, and the mine was closed in 1863. The quality of the coal was poor, and the quantity did not support further commercial mining at the site. The Pattle location's output contrasted with the slightly more productive yield that would eventually come from the Sehome Mine, a little less than two miles to the northeast.

SEHOME COAL MINE

Henry Brown and Samuel Hewitt were workers brought from San Francisco for Henry Roeder's lumber mill. They made their coal discovery on the east side of the bay, supposedly when they saw the coal exposed at the base of an uprooted tree on the bay side of Sehome Hill, near today's intersection of Laurel Street and Railroad Avenue. This finding led to the founding of the Bellingham Bay Coal Company in 1853 and the beginning of the Sehome Mine. Some digging began in 1853, though the Sehome Coal Mine actually opened in 1854. Investors believed that the mine would provide lignite coal for the expanding market for ship fuel, local heating and industrial uses.

The Sehome mine was dug under the city of Bellingham during the years 1854 to 1878, in approximately a rectangular area bounded by State Street, Cornwall Street, Laurel Street and Magnolia Street. Its exact dimensions and underground locations are unknown today. Maps of the mine were destroyed in the San Francisco earthquake and fires of 1906. Three mine entries were ultimately used, all very close together. Two were at the foot of Laurel, one at Laurel and Cornwall (1853) and the other at Laurel and Railroad Avenue (1859); the third was slightly to the south and west at the foot of Myrtle and Railroad Avenue. The mine tunnels were relatively close to the surface. In recent years, when engineers were studying the area under the southwest corner of Holly Street and Railroad Avenue for the development of a six-story parking garage, two shafts drilled vertically hit the mine tunnels at eighty-three feet and seventy-seven feet, thus ending the plans for a multilevel heavy parking lot over this area.

The first coal bunker—a pier to load coal onto ships from railroad cars, mostly headed for San Francisco—was built for the Sehome Coal Mine in 1859. It was sometimes called the Old Coal Wharf or the Sehome Wharf. Located at the foot of Pine Street, it occupied the space later taken by the southern tip of the Georgia Pacific Lumber Mill. This bunker was also the one initially used by the Blue Canyon Coal Mine for loading its coal onto ships in Bellingham Bay.

A second coal bunker was constructed at the foot of Beech Street. It was used briefly before yet another coal bunker was constructed at the foot of Bryant Street. The Bryant Street bunker was used by the Blue Canyon Mine after it opened in 1891. Thus, historically, there were three coal bunkers on the bay in Bellingham: at the foot of Cedar and Pine Streets (the first Sehome bunker), at the foot of Beech Street (the second Sehome bunker) and at the foot of Bryant Avenue (the Blue Canyon bunker).

By 1867, the Sehome mine was producing 1,400 tons of coal per month. Late in 1867, a fire in the mine required that it be flooded with water from Bellingham Bay to extinguish the flames. The mine remained flooded for almost a year before the water was pumped out. Later, yet another fire required repeat flooding, but mining was again resumed. The mine was worked for ten to eleven years thereafter, and production was reported to be 262 to 1,400 tons per month. The mine closed permanently in 1878, but its profitability encouraged coal mining elsewhere, including around Lake Whatcom.

Bellingham Coal Mine

The Bellingham Coal Mine was the most productive coal extraction business in the history of Whatcom County. The coal seams were thicker than at other locations in Whatcom County, the average being twelve feet, six inches. This mine was located about two miles northwest of the Sehome mine, south and slightly west of today's junction of I-5 and the Guide Meridian. The main entry to the mine sat approximately 800 feet directly to the west of the intersection of Birchwood Avenue and the Guide Meridian, at 1650 Birchwood Avenue, just beyond the south end of the Bellingham Country Club. The main shaft was directed to the southwest, and successively deeper levels progressed almost to the edge of Bellingham Bay. There were eleven

Bellingham Coal Mine. Surface structures and roads are depicted overlying the mine tunnels themselves. The tunnels were extensive. *Washington State Department of Natural Resources.*

levels, the first at about 300 feet from the entrance; the deepest was about 1,166 feet below the surface, underneath today's Bellingham Technical College. The levels were about 300 feet apart.

The mine operated by the room-and-pillar method. The coal was extensive, so the scale of extraction was large. Tunnels were bored from the main shaft laterally for great distances on both sides. Each lateral shaft was separated from the next by about three hundred to four hundred feet. It is estimated that there are about two hundred miles of tunnels in this mine. The rooms averaged twenty feet wide and seven feet high, and the pillars were thirty feet between rooms, rather typical for the room-and-pillar method. Two rails went into each room, one for incoming empty coal cars and one for cars full of about two tons of coal. Miners were paid by the ton, and they were expected to load about eight cars per shift. Men worked in pairs. Horses and mules pulled the railcars filled with coal; these animals spent their entire lives underground, with some of them "retiring" to the surface as they aged. Full stables were kept underground. Only in the 1940s did electric locomotives replace the animals.

The mine began operation in September 1918 under the Bellingham Bay Improvement Company, using the name Bellingham Coal Mine Company, and it continued production until 1951. In the early years of operation, the mine produced about two hundred thousand tons of coal per year. It was then sold to the Northwest Improvement Company; mining resumed in 1952.

The mine was closed permanently in 1955. The entrances were sealed, and water eventually filled most of the tunnels. It, too, in its early days influenced enthusiasm for coal mining around Lake Whatcom.

Blue Canyon Coal Mine

The date of the first coal discovery in the vicinity of Blue Canyon is disputed. Some say it was in 1858, while other reports have one Harry McCabe discovering the coal deposits in about 1873. The first serious exploration in the area of Blue Canyon Mine was in 1876, when the Bellingham Bay Coal Company discovered that there might be veins of coal sufficient for mining on the southeast end of Lake Whatcom. Initial assessments were not promising; the veins were too far from the surface, and it might take a mile of tunnels just to reach the deposits. In addition, tunnels for air circulation for the safety of the miners could add enormously to the cost. Furthermore, any coal mined there at that time would have been difficult to transport to market. Nevertheless, a mine opening was begun. However, little was accomplished, and the mining efforts ceased. Thoughts of digging for coal there were abandoned.

In the first survey of the area by Oliver B. Iverson in 1883, he noted a "shanty" (likely a primitive cabin) and a "coal dump" at the northwest corner of Section 22 of Township 37 N, Range 4 E. Clearly someone had already been digging for coal in this region around Lake Whatcom.

Interest in mining in the area was rejuvenated again in 1883–85. A group of men from the Tacoma area saw the potential for a business at Lake Whatcom when the land was surveyed and opened for claims, both for homesteading and mining. These men began digging a tunnel in 1886, higher on the hill than the previous site, but they were unsuccessful in establishing a productive mine. Also, the treasurer of the Tacoma group apparently disappeared the same day that the money they'd collected for the project vanished. Subsequently, others claimed the land because of abandonment of prior claims. Legal wrangling involved the courts and local land officers, as well as the Department of the Interior.

The major Blue Canyon coal seam was discovered in 1887 in Sections 15 and 22, Township 37 N, Range 4 E. Most coal would come from Section 15. Bloedel received his patent for a section of land there in 1890–91. Clarence W. Carter acquired adjacent land in 1891–92.

The Blue Canyon Coal Mining Company was incorporated on December 16, 1889, with James F. Wardner as president; Edward C. Gove as vice president; Bloedel as business manager, secretary and developer; and Donovan as general superintendent and director of the mine. Donovan also oversaw the barges used to transport the coal to Silver Beach and the subsequent delivery to Bellingham Bay. Wardner was hands-off; he fully delegated the operation of the mine to Bloedel and Donovan. Allegedly, Wardner had named the site Blue Canyon one autumn day because of the consistent blue haze over this end of Lake Whatcom.

One investor, J.F. McNaught, who was associated with the Northern Pacific Railroad, put $100,000 into the company with either the implicit or explicit agreement that the Northern Pacific would provide rail service for the coal southward through Park and Wickersham to Anacortes.

Actual mining began on about November 15, 1890, with ten men, soon expanding to forty employees. At the beginning of the mining, the land itself was owned by James Wardner, E.C. Gove, C.W. Carter and Julius Bloedel.

On January 3, 1891, new officers were announced for the company: Wardner as president, J.F. McNaught as vice president, C.W. Carter as treasurer and Bloedel as secretary. The officers proposed that they build a steamer to tow barges filled with coal to the northwesternmost point of Lake Whatcom, where the coal would be offloaded onto wagons to be pulled along an envisioned road from the start of Whatcom Creek to Bellingham Bay. At this early date, February 1891, some company officials believed that the BB&BC Railroad would build a line from Bellingham Bay to the mine along the north and east banks of Lake Whatcom, though Wardner continued to assert that the coal would be transported through Anacortes via the Northern Pacific. Furthermore, company officers claimed that the main offices for Blue Canyon would also be located in Anacortes. This outcome never materialized, as on September 25, 1891, the final decision was made that the coal would be shipped through Bellingham Bay.

In 1891, the first opening of the mine was made in the southeast quarter of Section 15; it was 1,123 feet above sea level, or 806 feet above the surface of Lake Whatcom. The technique used was room-and-pillar mining. (The second opening would be made much later, located on the border between Sections 15 and 22, roughly 1,750 feet west of the first opening, at about 658 feet above the level of Lake Whatcom.) The coal seams varied greatly in thickness—the largest being up to forty feet—but they averaged seven to twelve feet. The coal was fine-grained and relatively soft bituminous coal, making it difficult to handle, as it crumbled easily. Coals are classified by their

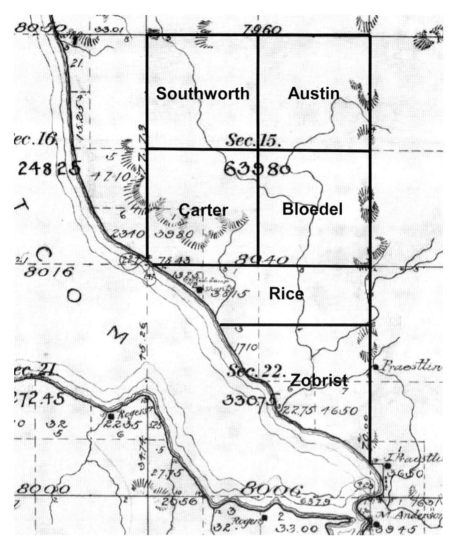

Original landholders in the area around Blue Canyon Mine and Blue Canyon City. The town of Blue Canyon would eventually occupy primarily the area of the Fred Zobrist claim. Coal rights were granted to J.H. Bloedel and C.W. Carter on April 1, 1891. They had actually begun developing the land and coal mine before final title and rights were granted. The Carter/Bloedel land would become the Blue Canyon Coal Company; C.E. Rice's property would become the Whatcom County Coal Company in about 1908. *Adapted from United States Bureau of Land Management.*

carbon content: anthracite (the highest heating value, but rare), bituminous, sub-bituminous and lignite. The carbon content reflects the age of the coal, lignite being the youngest. Furthermore, lower carbon content correlates with high moisture and crumbling that makes coal difficult to process and transport. The Blue Canyon coal had to be washed at the upper workings, and pieces were rarely larger than about seven inches in diameter. The Blue Canyon Coal Company produced three distinct varieties of coal: domestic or house coal, gas coal and steam coal. Blue Canyon coal emitted a slightly higher heat content, 11,919 BTU/pound, compared to the Bellingham Mines No. 1 and No. 2, at 10,542-11,048 BTU/pound. When used as gas-producing coal, the Blue Canyon product yielded 12,096 cubic feet of gas per ton of coal, a very good output. When used to heat water to produce steam, Blue Canyon coal evaporated 10.09 pounds of water per pound of coal, compared to Seattle coal at 4.14 pounds of water per pound of coal and Cardiff English coal at 13.12 pounds of water per pound of coal.

The geology of the region around Blue Canyon made coal mining treacherous; it was more difficult than anticipated. The area was prone to landslides, and it seemed that the entire face of the mountain where the openings were located was moving downward toward the edge of Lake Whatcom in a process referred to as land slips—not precisely landslides but with the same end result. The openings to the mine would shift downward and cause the early portions of the tunnels to collapse.

By February 27, 1891, the tram from the mine entrance had been completed, approximately two thousand feet long and descending eight hundred feet to the edge of the water of Lake Whatcom. On March 3, 1891, the contract was let for the tiny steamship *Geneva* to tow the coal across Lake Whatcom to the Silver Beach area. On March 9, 1891, two wagons, each pulled by four horses, came to Bellingham Bay with the first delivery of coal from the Blue Canyon mine, described as "sacks" of coal—indicating that the delivery was more a grandstanding maneuver than it was practical. None other than J.J. Donovan himself ceremoniously drove one of these wagons. The arrival of the wagons in New Whatcom was a spectacular event. The coal was long-awaited, and the coal wagons were gloriously decorated. Citizens in the area were desperate for the local business ventures to succeed and stimulate economic growth in the region. By March 16, only one week after the first shipment, Bloedel was touting the production of forty to fifty tons per day.

James F. Wardner met with M.E. Downs, an associate of Jay Gould, in May 1891, leading to the formation of an investment group in Helena,

Montana, that would play heavily in the future of Blue Canyon. By July 3, 1891, Wardner had announced that Blue Canyon had been sold, though the specifics of the sale were unknown. Peter Larson was a prime investor in this group, variably called the Montana Syndicate or the Helena Syndicate. Even during these negotiations, by July 12, the Blue Canyon Coal Company was well underway. Bloedel reported that the company was ready to build a railroad to the site, as well as coal bunkers on Bellingham Bay. Everything was moving quickly. The deal adding investors to the Blue Canyon Coal Mining Company was begun on July 18, 1891, and completed on July 31, 1891, at a meeting in Portland, Oregon. Bloedel and Donovan each bought into the company. In September 1891, these new investors came for an inspection. Wardner completed the sale of his interest in the mine. Another restructuring of the company made M.E. Downs president, Bloedel secretary and Donovan construction superintendent.

The land on which the town of Blue Canyon would be situated passed through many hands before the town actually appeared. The first owner

The Blue Canyon Coal Mine. The *Ella* is depicted in the foreground towing a coal barge. Sketch by Eva (Reasoner) Siemons. *Whatcom Museum, Sk1977.0065.000004.*

of the land that would become the town of Blue Canyon—land slightly farther south in Section 22—was Fred Zobrist, who bought 166.35 acres from the government on August 24, 1891, under the Land Act of 1820. This transaction was finalized on December 11, 1891. The first residents were the Zobrist family. The Blue Canyon townsite would be platted as nearly seventy-five acres, slightly to the south and bordering on the edge of the mines themselves. The bulk of the coal mine itself would ultimately be located under Section 15. Apparently, Zobrist had purchased a "preemption" claim from Clarence W. Carter and his wife, Anna, for $1,000 in 1889. A preemption claim was a right of first refusal to purchase the land from the government at a minimum price. Squatters on land—likely the Carters had settled on it and made some improvements—often claimed this preemption right and were allowed to sell this claim to someone else. Subsequently, the Blue Canyon Townsite Corporation (Julius Bloedel, C.E. Rice, C.L. Erwin and E.C. Gove) bought 74.85 acres from Zobrist for a total of $9,000 on January 13, 1891. The town plat provided the legal approval to construct roads, a railroad, a water system, electrical lines and telegraph lines. Zobrist retained the rest of the land, though he gave Bloedel and the corporation the rights to the timber. The sale of the townsite included the mineral rights underneath it. Zobrist also sold a piece of land one mile long for a mere $250 to accommodate the anticipated railway that had been proposed. The right-of-way for the railroad (called Railroad Avenue) was one hundred feet wide; streets themselves in Blue Canyon City were fifty feet wide.

The townsite incorporation was written on March 23, 1891, and it was filed on May 4, 1891. Only a few days later, newspapers ran large ads calling Blue Canyon the "Pittsburgh of Bellingham Bay." Blue Canyon City represented the "chances of a lifetime" to purchase prize lots for homebuilding. The organizers even aggressively projected August 1 as the day that the railroad would complete its line into Blue Canyon. The Blue Canyon Townsite Company (financially and organizationally distinct from the Blue Canyon Mining Company) sold the lots in the seventy-five-acre town for fifty, seventy-five and one hundred dollars, with half to be paid down in cash and one-quarter due at four and eight months. Ads promoted the coal and timber industries that would soon flourish in the area. Land speculation was underway.

Blue Canyon City developed rapidly, but not always in a manner acceptable to everyone. By August 22, 1891, a saloon had been built. By 1892, there were about forty students in the Blue Canyon School. Soon, the post office

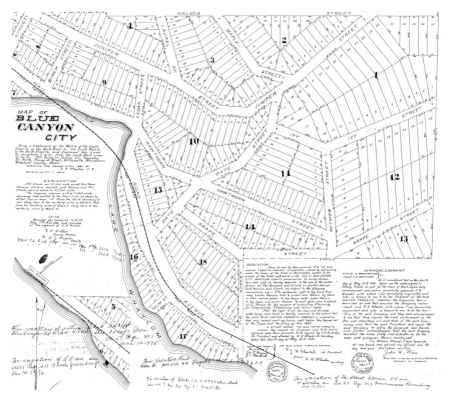

Plat map of Blue Canyon City, established May 4, 1891. The railroad along the shore is listed as the Seattle, Lake Shore and Eastern Railway, though the Bellingham Bay & Eastern Railroad was the rail line actually constructed here. What was drawn initially on a map was not necessarily what would ultimately be built. *Whatcom County Tax Parcel Viewer.*

in Park closed, and one in Blue Canyon opened. A boardinghouse and hotel soon appeared. Blue Canyon City was the quintessential company town.

By July 1892, the coal mine and its early transportation system were effectively operational. On July 1, 1892, Donovan celebrated his success with a party at Silver Beach with 150 guests. Coal output would rapidly increase, and by November 1892, the mine was producing five hundred tons per day.

From 1891 to 1893, travel from Blue Canyon to New Whatcom often involved the stage from Blue Canyon to Wickersham; the Seattle, Lake Shore and Eastern Railroad to Sumas; and then the Bellingham Bay and British Columbia Railroad to New Whatcom. It was a circuitous and time-consuming route.

In the early days, miners worked one of two ten-hour shifts per day and made about $2.50 to $3.25 per day. Their pay was dependent on the number of tons of coal they extracted. The miners could rent space in the local boarding/rooming house for $4.75 per week. The annual output of the mine then was about ten thousand to thirty thousand tons.

Bringing the coal to market was a challenge. The coal was mined and delivered to the surface in small railcars, either hand-pushed or drawn by mules or horses. It was then delivered by tram to the Blue Canyon bunker at the edge of Lake Whatcom. From there, it was loaded in piles onto barges or, later, into railcars and carried to Silver Beach. One barge could transport twenty-four coal cars, and barges were often towed by the steamboat *Ella*. These coal cars could be transferred directly to the rails at Silver Beach, the dock for which was located close to where Bloedel-Donovan Park and the Old Mill Village sit today.

The coal wharf at Silver Beach had three aprons to transfer the railroad cars filled with coal from the barge to the wharf. The surface of the wharf was nearly at water level to facilitate the transfer of the railcars. The barge being constructed at Thompson's Mill in Geneva by G.B. Peavey in Seattle was to have three sets of tracks, hence the need for three aprons. The wharf at Silver Beach was 160 feet long by 36 feet wide and had three sets of parallel tracks for the three rows of cars, eight cars on each track. The cars were relatively small for railcars, and they had only four wheels each. Each car held 10 tons of coal, so the payload for the entire barge was 240 tons. These cars, built by the Fairhaven Foundry and Machine Company, were painted blue with black lettering, identifying them as belonging to the Blue Canyon Mine. Bloedel estimated that the value of the cargo of coal in a single trip would be about $10,000, so the barge was constructed for maximum safety. There were nine floating, airtight, independent compartments supporting the entire structure, so if one or a few were punctured, the barge would remain afloat.

Initially, rail transport of the coal from the wharf at the north end of Lake Whatcom to Bellingham Bay used Blue Canyon's own short spur to the tracks of the electric trolley to Electric Avenue, Lake Street (Lakeway Drive), Woburn Street and then Kentucky Street. The maximum grade along this route was 4.9 percent, a considerable incline for any available locomotive.

The first coal to be transported from the Blue Canyon mine *by rail* from the Lake Whatcom barge and pier to Bellingham Bay was delivered in June or July 1892 (the exact reported date varies). At the outset, four twenty-five-ton cars, loaded by hand with shovels at the edge of Silver Beach, brought Blue Canyon coal to the Sehome bunker at the edge of Bellingham Bay. Successfully hauling this load was never a foregone conclusion—it was always tenuous whether the

Coal bunker at Blue Canyon Mine, looking north, 1891–92, before the railroad had come to Blue Canyon. The boat barely visible on the left is the *Ella. Whatcom Museum 1996.0010.003376.*

Barge on Lake Whatcom carrying coal cars from Blue Canyon coal mine, July 27, 1898. *University of Washington Special Collections, Photo by L. Heath, Industries and Occupations Subject Files, PH Coll 1294, IND0339, #UW26223z.*

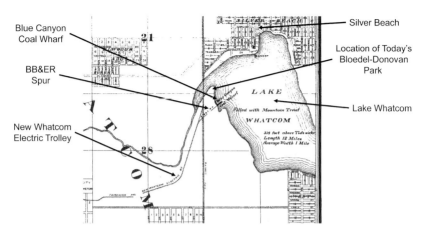

Wharf for Blue Canyon coal before the Bellingham Bay and Eastern Railroad (BB&ER) was completed around Lake Whatcom. A short spur of the railroad connected to the trolley line. This wharf, about two hundred feet long, was used mostly from 1891 to June 8, 1892, when the railroad was completed around the lake. *Map of Fairhaven and Vicinity, Edmund S. Hincks, 1892, Miscellaneous Map Collection, Maps of Bellingham, Folder 4-10, CPNWS.*

locomotives would have sufficient power to bring such a load over the hills between Lake Whatcom and the bay. At Silver Beach, the coal was transferred to a spur of the BB&E Railroad that connected to the electric trolley line for transport to Bellingham. (The Silver Beach wharf was used from 1891 to June 8, 1892, when the BB&E Railroad was completed around the east and north side of Lake Whatcom.) The coal was subsequently taken to the bunkers at Bellingham Bay, initially the Sehome Dock.

The officers of the Blue Canyon Mine contracted with A.L. McCoy & Company (subcontracted to Davey and Gibson) to build huge coal bunkers south of the Sehome Wharf at Bellingham Bay, north of today's Boulevard Park, at Bryant Avenue at Elk (now State) Street. It would use more than 700 piles, each 80 feet long, and more than 800,000 feet of timber. The rails were 47 feet above the high-water mark. Construction of this pier required 39,120 pounds of nails, screws, bolts, washers and rods. The wharf itself was 40 feet wide and 153 feet long. The bunkers had 14 pockets for coal, lined with a total of 18,000 pounds of galvanized iron, a "Miller patent" chute, and the bunkers would hold more than 1,500 tons of coal when full. Optimists estimated that three trainloads of coal would be delivered to the bunker daily. Until this bunker was completed, Blue Canyon used the Sehome wharf. (Fortunately for the yet-to-emerge Bloedel-Donovan-Larson timber industry, the Blue Canyon Coal Company constructed its coal bunkers in the bay with the capacity to handle huge logs as well.) When the railroad was developed, the coal was deposited directly into railcars at the Blue Canyon bunker and then transported by rail the entire distance to Bellingham Bay.

Labor disputes also arose soon after the mine was opened. On August 29, 1891, the workers struck because they believed that they were being shortchanged. Their pay averaged $3.00 per day, with a supplement of $5.00 per week for room and board. In addition, they had to expend considerable time and energy walking to and from work up and down a steep path. They claimed that this trek alone was worth $1.50 per day.

Early in the history of the Blue Canyon Coal Mine, it was not clear that the mine would be profitable. In March 1894, the owners of the mine had to decrease miners' pay, and they were fearful that the miners would quit en masse. Nearly simultaneously, however, the United States Navy ship *Yorktown* arrived in the Bellingham harbor. There it loaded some coal from the Blue Canyon bunker. The future of the Blue Canyon mine might have rested on the analysis of the quality of this coal. The *Yorktown* skipper reported that the coal was as good as that obtained in Canada; the mine was saved. The Blue Canyon mine soon became the primary source of coal for the U.S. Navy's Pacific fleet. Some coal went to San Francisco and Vancouver; some went to the town of Concrete for the processing of cement. Furthermore, local sale for business and residential heating was conducted at the bunkers on East Elk Street. Furnace coal sold for three dollars per ton.

Mining from Blue Canyon was concentrated on two separate workings. The original opening was called the Slope, and it descended at thirty degrees for about 1,000 feet, with four levels of tunnels accessing coal seams. This first portal was 806 feet above the level of Lake Whatcom, and the second was at an altitude of 658 feet above Lake Whatcom's surface (Lake Whatcom itself was 317 feet above sea level). The first portal descended into the hillside about 600 feet before encountering the first coal seam. Structures around the opening of the Slope were extensive: a fan house, an engine room, a boiler house, a blacksmith shop, stables, a storeroom, an oil house and a bathhouse, where miners could take either cold or hot showers after a day at work. Nearby was a boardinghouse, a bunkhouse and multiple small cabins where men lived. Other mine entrances (openings) would come later.

The small cars that worked the innards of the mine each held two tons of coal, pulled by mules within the tunnels. As they exited the mine opening, the cars would be attached to a cable that lowered them along the tram to the bunker that straddled the railway at the edge of Lake Whatcom. The weight of a loaded car pulled an empty car back up to the mine opening. Brakes on the cable controlled the loaded car's speed of descent. At the

The original Sehome bunker was located near the end of Cedar and Pine Streets and was used to load both Sehome Mine and Blue Canyon Mine coal onto ships on the bay (circa 1880–90). The bunker pictured here was also a combination of Sehome and Blue Canyon Mine interests, and it was located just south of the foot of Bryant Street (circa 1892–1904). It was demolished in May 1904. This structure is also occasionally called the Sehome bunker, though most references call it the Blue Canyon bunker. Note that there was a ramp that was capable of handling huge logs, dumping them into the water, a provision that would accommodate the burgeoning timber industry. *Biery Papers, #2791, CPNWS.*

bunker, coal was separated through a series of three screens to divide the contents of the car into coal lumps of different sizes, and then the coal was washed. In 1893, at the peak of the mine's production, Blue Canyon Coal Mine employed more than one hundred men and had a monthly payroll of $12,000 to $15,000. Its peak capacity was five hundred tons per day.

Safety was always a major issue for the Blue Canyon Mine, with each man working a grueling eight-hour or a ten-hour shift. One of the first accidents at the Blue Canyon mine occurred on August 7, 1891, when a firedamp (methane) explosion at 325 feet into a shaft burned superintendent P.J. Commiskey and treasurer M.E. Downs. Both were taken to the Sisters' Hospital (later called St. Joseph's Hospital) in Sehome. Their burns were not life-threatening, but the accident highlighted the need for better air circulation in the mine and a better means of detecting explosive gases. Soon thereafter, on November 1, 1891, two other men (W.L.F. Suiter and Chris Allen) were killed when a boiler fell on them. In August 1892, two

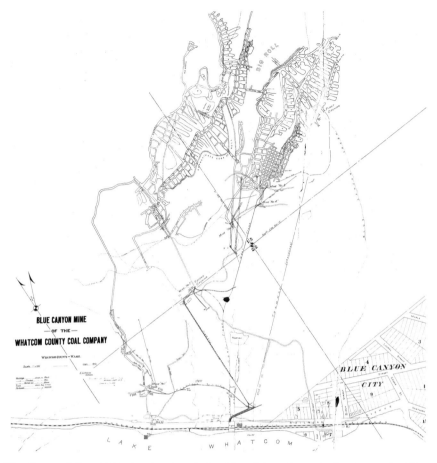

Blue Canyon Mine, 1914, showing the relationships of the mine to the bunkers and to Blue Canyon City. *Washington State Department of Natural Resources*.

men were seriously injured while working in an area where the ventilation fan had been malfunctioning; methane ignited, and they suffered burns. In November 1892, workers lost control of a coal car being lowered on the tram as the car was traveling toward the bunker. The car struck a worker, hurtling him forty-eight feet onto the rocks below. He suffered a fractured skull and spine, and he died six hours later. On January 3, 1893, the coal bunker foreman J.A. McGhee was killed when his clothing was caught in machinery he was oiling, pulling him into the apparatus and crushing him. Later in 1893, an explosion injured one miner; a cave-in killed yet another. In November 1893, another worker received injuries to his leg when a car in which he was riding failed to stop at the top of the tram, smashing into

Blue Canyon Mine entrance. *Biery Papers, #2774, CPNWS.*

the bulkhead at the entry to the mine. In January 1895, another miner was badly burned by a firedamp explosion. At one point, the local newspaper the *Reveille* tallied nine serious accidents at the mine over a couple of years, not counting the minor ones. This mining was quite dangerous.

However, the mine would soon experience yet additional problems. As the workers tunneled further and further into the hillside at Blue Canyon, they encountered more and more firedamp—methane that was explosive. They installed huge fans to ventilate the tunnels, but these proved insufficient. The underground passages were extensive. Tunnels within the hillside were thousands of feet long. Fresh air simply would not circulate adequately in these shafts and tunnels.

The state mine inspector visited the mine five times in 1895. The original opening into the mine had been abandoned because all the coal had been extracted from that seam. The "new mine" had been recently opened about 350 feet above lake level. Ventilation had been better in the original mine entry, and some miners complained that ventilation at the new mine was not as good as it had been at the previous site. The inspector made only minor suggestions for the improvement of safety, but he agreed that the ventilation at the new mine was insufficient. A subsequent visit confirmed that all his suggestions had been followed.

The methane problem at this new mine was recognized all too acutely on March 28, 1895. Donovan and three employees experienced an explosion in the early portion of the mine near the entrance, but there were no injuries. Precautions were enhanced against further such accidents. Nevertheless, at 2:45 p.m. on April 8, 1895, a huge explosion again occurred in the mine. Twenty-five men were underground in eight rooms. Seven men were killed immediately by the blast, and sixteen others died of asphyxiation as they were trapped in the tunnels. No fire followed the explosion, but rescue efforts, in general, were futile. Mine safety regulations at the time were much less rigid than they are today. They required that fans exchange one hundred cubic feet of air per man per minute; today, that requirement is three thousand to thirty thousand cubic feet of air per man per minute. The ventilation fans had been running, but the tunnel into the mountainside was eight hundred feet long, with another tunnel extending laterally one thousand feet, opening into twenty-six rooms where mining was underway. All miners were using safety lamps. Since the explosion occurred just before a shift change, the group of miners heading toward the mine opening was immediately able to initiate rescue efforts, but they were successful only in retrieving bodies.

Immediately on hearing about the explosion, both Julius Bloedel and J.J. Donovan rushed to the scene on special trains provided by the BB&E Railroad, taking them to Silver Beach. They brought three physicians and ten off-duty miners to Blue Canyon to assist in search, recovery and treatment of the injured. Bloedel and the physicians and miners were unable to retrieve any survivors beyond the two (James Kerns and Edward T. Gellum) who had already escaped. Twenty-three men had perished. This tragedy was one of the worst accidents in the history of Washington mine safety.

Coffins were quickly constructed, and initial services were held for the twenty-three men at the Blue Canyon School. Then their bodies were transported to the north end of the lake by the steamers *Ella*, *Emma D*, *Thistle* and *Regie*.

An inquest was begun immediately. On April 10, Washington State mine inspector David Edmunds testified about his findings. Contrary to the off-the-record statements about poor ventilation, all witnesses testified that the air circulation was good and that it would have been good even if there had been more miners in the tunnels at the time. One experienced miner who wanted to remain anonymous reported rather fatalistically to a writer for the Seattle *Post-Intelligencer* after the explosion that "as long as there are coal mines and as long as the people use coal there will be accidents and occasional great loss of life." The investigation concluded that the deaths of the twenty-three men were not caused by company negligence. However, Edmunds, in a later report, said that a dynamite charge had been inappropriately set, causing the methane gas to ignite. Edwards asked Donovan to replace the assistant superintendent of the mine. He threatened that if Donovan did not comply, he would close the mine. Donovan complied, and the man was fired. Strangely, though Donovan kept a rather extensive personal diary throughout his entire life, this mine explosion and its aftermath were not recorded in it.

The miners were all buried in the Bay View Cemetery, with more than 1,500 members of the Bellingham community in attendance. Bloedel erected a monument to the twenty-three deceased miners, and it stands to this day.

Work resumed at the mine on April 17, and by April 20, Blue Canyon was once again operating at full force.

The Blue Canyon Mine had never become the bonanza its investors wanted it to be. The coal became less abundant in about 1897, and labor disputes further affected the productivity of the mine. Bloedel himself replaced M.E. Downs as president of the company, but in 1897, Bloedel resigned because of difficulty in the mining operations and his belief that the mine would not become profitable again. Donovan, however, thought the mine still had some useful life remaining, and his optimism would support it in years to come.

By April 1899, the mine's workforce was again at forty men, but its output was only about fifty tons per day. Problems continued to plague the operation. On December 4, 1900, the coal barge capsized, throwing ten of the cars into the lake, dumping one hundred tons of coal into about eighteen feet of water.

In 1903, the mine was still officially owned by the Montana Syndicate. About 1903, the miners began to want to unionize, becoming a problem for the management. The mine briefly closed in 1903.

In November 1904, Donovan once again tried to open the mining operations at Blue Canyon. Donovan went to Helena on his way back from an East Coast trip and tried to convince the owners of the Helena Syndicate that mining should be resumed. A new vein of coal encouraged them, but reinvestment lagged.

The Blue Canyon mine was run from 1904 to 1907 under owner J.W. Lawton as a reorganized entity with many different lease agreements and managements. Production was sporadic.

However, in 1907, J.J. Donovan again thought it might be possible to resurrect the Blue Canyon Mine. The initial cost of its opening had been about $45,000 in 1891; nearly $500,000 worth of coal had been extracted from the mine before 1903. After 1903, production was only about one hundred tons per month. Donovan once again encouraged investment in the mine, but it was going to require different mining methods and considerable investment. In effect, the mining operation needed to be started from scratch because the tunnels initially dug into the hillside were unstable.

In 1907, the Seattle Lighting Company bought the Blue Canyon Coal Company and renamed it the Whatcom County Mining Company. About fifty men worked the tunnels. Coal shipments to Bellingham Bay resumed in September 1907. Most of the small yield from the mine from 1907 to 1919 went to Seattle to fuel the Seattle Gas Works, but the output was only fifty to seventy-five tons per day.

The Blue Canyon mine was closed permanently in October–November 1919. The final sealing of the last mine shaft was completed in late 1921. The Whatcom County Coal Company was dissolved on March 13, 1922.

An analysis decades later, in 1961, estimated that there were still 44 million tons of bituminous coal remaining at Blue Canyon Mine. By the time of its demise, it had produced 280,000 tons of coal.

Beginning around 1903, the population center of Blue Canyon gradually moved south and east to the village of Park, only about one mile away. By 1906, even the Blue Canyon school had been disassembled and reassembled—in a new design—at Park. Thus, the town of Park began to reform.

In 1904, the Northern Pacific Railroad had begun to dismantle the coal bunkers on Bellingham Bay. Having been in place about twelve years, the timbers were beginning to age ungracefully (the average pier on Bellingham Bay lasted for even less than twelve years). Once the timbers were dismantled, they were burned.

More detailed reports later examined why the Blue Canyon Coal Mine had failed. Geologic records stated, "The irregularity of the thickness of the coal seam, the soft character of it, and of its walls; the presence of bad gas, the caving and sliding nature of the formation, the presence of rolls and faults, and the difficulties encountered in surface sliding, all were factors in making the mining practically impossible to continue on a commercial basis. [However,] the composition of the coal and its coking property always made it attractive in spite of the difficulties."[*]

* Jenkins, *Geological Investigation*, 104.

The coal bunker at Blue Canyon itself burned on July 20–21, 1920, after a Northern Pacific train's sparks ignited the flammable structure. It was completely destroyed.

While coal mining was on the decline, land use turned to lumbering. The bulk of the Blue Canyon Coal Mine site was sold to the E.K. Wood Lumber Company on September 28, 1922. Wood sold it to Soundview Pulp Company on January 14, 1941; Soundview Pulp merged with Scott Paper Company in stages, one on November 13, 1951, and one on August 30, 1954.

The initial success of the Blue Canyon Coal Mine, as well as the productivity of other coal mines in the Bellingham area, fueled enthusiasm for other coal mines in Whatcom County, especially around Lake Whatcom. One had only to report an initial finding of a tiny sample of coal for investors to rush to put money into ventures that otherwise might have seemed too risky. Many sites around Lake Whatcom became foci of such attention.

GLEN ECHO COAL MINE

Coal was discovered at Glen Echo in 1896, but diggings began only in 1918. The Glen Echo Coal Mining Company was founded in 1920, with M.L. Dickerson as the president and Andrew Ecklund as the superintendent. Glen Echo (also briefly called the Blue Flame Mine) was located at the headwaters of Anderson Creek.[*] (An older mine, sometimes called the Raper Mine, was located about one mile to the north-northeast of the second opening.) The largest Glen Echo coal seam was about five feet thick, with some subsidiary seams three to four feet thick. Overall, there were five different small seams. The room-and-pillar mining technique was used. The coal was processed, graded and washed locally; storage bunkers were present on-site.

The mine was worked from 1920 to 1948, but its output was small. For example, in 1921, it reported producing 618 tons, but by 1932, the mine only yielded 18 tons of coal for the entire year. The average year's output was about 2,000 tons, ranging from 18 to 9,376 tons. The overall quality of the ore was rather poor. The BTU per pound output from the coal was 9,715, compared to Blue Canyon coal at 11,919 BTU/pound and the Bellingham Mines No. 1 and No. 2 at 10,542–11,048 BTU/pound.

---

[*] At the common corner of Sections 5 and 9, Township 38 North, Range 4 East.

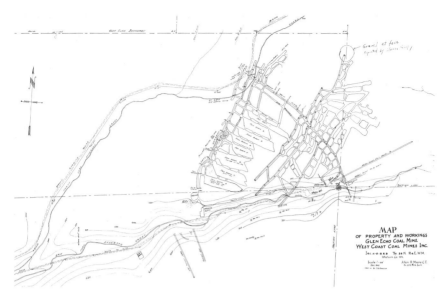

Glen Echo Mine, 1942. *Washington State Department of Natural Resources.*

By the end of its life, the mine had yielded a total of about sixty-five thousand tons. Its demise was caused by decreasing production, the diminishing size of the coal seam and the presence of glacial gravel, which interrupted the coal seam. In addition to the marginal thickness of the coal seam, the seam itself was almost vertical, and the height of the tunnel had to be quite low, making mining difficult.

A portion of the Glen Echo Mine property is now Glen Echo Garden, a botanical site that also supports resident artists and hosts social events.

Geneva Coal Mine

The Geneva coal mine was first owned by Isaac N. Orchard, who bought 160 acres at this site on November 16, 1891.* The coal in Geneva was discovered long before any serious mining began there. A coal seam was reported in August 1891, ranging in thickness from eighteen inches to five feet. Later, it was analyzed to be as good in quality as the coal from Blue Canyon. However, its energy output was low at 7,161 BTU/pound, compared to Blue Canyon at 11,919. It was a long time before the mine itself became active, opening in 1921.

---

* NE ¼ SW ¼, Section 34, Township 38 North, Range 3 East.

The mine entrance was about one mile from Lake Whatcom, and the tunnel to the coal seam measured 350 feet long. The coal seam there was only 28–29 inches thick. After removal from the mine, the coal was sent down a 2,800-foot skid road to bunkers located next to Geneva Road. A second entrance was attempted about 250 feet from the first and 68 feet lower. It also yielded little.

The Geneva Coal Mine opened briefly in 1921 under the name Pacific Atomized Fuel Company. The president was Otho H. Williams, and the secretary-treasurer was James L. Gilfilen. The Pacific Atomized Fuel Company had been locally incorporated on January 30, 1920. At the same time, another similar company was incorporated, the Bellingham Atomized Fuel Company. A process for "atomizing" coal would be used, allegedly taking low-grade coal and treating it to give it higher burning qualities. Such a plant was to be built in Bellingham. The process involved initially crushing coal into "grain particles" smaller than the size of a pea, then extracting moisture from the mixture. The coal was then further pulverized to the consistency of flour, and allegedly its heating quality was increased ten- to twentyfold. Furthermore, coal treated in this manner was easier to control, since addition or injection of this powdery substance to a fire could be adjusted with precision, in contrast to adding lumps of coal to a fire. Other such plants were operating elsewhere in the United States. Otho Williams was a trusted name in the community because he had been the pastor of the First Christian Church of Bellingham. This venture seemed to be legitimate. But hardship was about to strike.

The Geneva mine had actually been in operation for a few weeks before its opening was reported to the public. Its coal was advertised as "high grade." The second vein there was nine feet thick. Both veins were close to the surface of the ground. By February 22, 1922, the Pacific Atomized Fuel Company had thirty-six men on its payroll, split between Geneva and Silver Beach, where they had another mine. In 1921, the total output for the Pacific Atomized Fuel Company was about 150 tons.

This mine was not very productive overall, yielding only a total of 350 tons of coal over the years 1921 to 1922. Like many businesses in Whatcom County at the time, the Pacific Atomized Fuel Company fell on hard times. On September 26, 1922, Tom Boyce (otherwise spelled Voyce), an employee of the company, filed a complaint against the Reverend Otho Williams, alleging grand larceny. Williams was arrested the same day. Boyce alleged that he had invested $800 in stock in the company, and that not only did Williams not give him the stock, but the company also had no tangible assets. Furthermore, Boyce claimed that many of the miners had been paid with promises of stock rather than cash. When the men later demanded either the balance of their cash or their stock certificates, Williams refused to produce either. Williams was given one day to secure a $1,000 bail bond; to employ a lawyer, if he wanted one; and to enter a plea of guilty or not guilty. Williams had claimed that he was part of a Chicago corporation, that he owned 1,200 acres of coal property and that the men would become part of that company by their "investment." Indeed, Williams had struck a deal with the Atomized Fuel Company, but it required him to prove acquisition of $500,000 in assets by July 1922, in return for which he could use the patented atomizing process if he paid the parent company a royalty. Time had expired for Williams to generate such assets. He had an option to buy the Silver Beach mining property, but in fact, he never owned it. Boyce charged that Williams had taken his money "by trick, fraud, and device." At that time, the Pacific Atomized Fuel Company had no real assets.

Williams was given a court date of October 7, 1922, and he told the prosecuting attorney that he would plead not guilty. However, on October 7, as reported in the *Bellingham Herald*, William entered a demurrer, a statement alleging that Boyce's charging documents for the court case did not conform to the legal requirements of the Washington State code, that more than one crime was alleged (at that time, in Whatcom County, only one crime was allowed in a charging document), that the facts did not constitute a crime and that "the information contains facts which if true would be a bar to the action." In other words, Williams tried to escape the charges on technicalities. Thereafter, the case seemed to disappear without fanfare. The mine itself slipped into obscurity.

The site of the Geneva Coal Mine corresponds today to the land to the southwest of the corner of Euclid Street and Eighth Street, adjacent to the Galbraith Mountain biking trails. It was sold to the City of Bellingham in 2004 for $4 million.

Rocky Ridge Coal Mine

Rocky Ridge Coal Mine was located on the southwest side of Lake Whatcom.* The first load of coal from Rocky Ridge—three tons—was delivered to Bellingham Bay on December 24, 1891. On February 27, 1892, a large contingent of dignitaries went from New Whatcom and Fairhaven

---

* SW ¼, Section 31, Township 38 North, Range 4 East.

to the mine, ferried on the *Regie* and the *Rose* and on a barge towed behind. Machinery was present and ready to begin work, and the *Fairhaven Herald* reported that the mine had "an enormous quantity of first-class coal in sight." The family of Colonel Harry A. Moore, the mine operator, held a grand party for these guests (and potential investors) with food, drink and music. At that time, the mine had a main shaft extending seventy-five feet into the hillside; was equipped with an engine and a boiler; and had a hoisting apparatus that pulled coal to the surface, about one hundred feet from the edge of the lake. From the mine opening, the coal slid down a chute to the wharf at the side of the lake.

The *Bellingham Bay Express* reported on March 14, 1893, that the mine would be opened in the spring. It said, "the veins have been prospected for a distance of about six miles and found in paying colors all the way." Perhaps this description was simply a ruse to boost the sale of stock in the company, because it also said, "More stock has been sold in the mine during the past month, and the outlook is unusually bright."

Some initial operations did indeed begin in 1892, but the mine was not fully developed until the turn of the century. Moore was not able to organize its mining successfully until 1903. The National Coal and Iron Company was formed to begin the process. The main shaft was said to be six hundred feet deep, and rails were ready to be put into position in the tunnel in November 1903. Newspapers reported that the company expected to be shipping coal by January 1904, employing two hundred men. Sadly, that prediction would never come to pass. Perhaps a few loads of coal were sent to Bellingham, but the Rocky Ridge Coal Mine never proved to be a commercial success.

The first opening—tunnel no. 1, on vein no. 3 of 5—was only 4 feet above the level of Lake Whatcom, about 500 feet to the west of the shore at Rocky Ridge Landing. The second opening—tunnel no. 2, also on vein no. 3—was 250 feet west of the landing and 10 feet above lake level. Analysis of the Rocky Ridge coal showed that its output was low at 7,232 BTU/pound, compared to Blue Canyon at 11,919 BTU/pound. Even though its quality was inferior to that of the Blue Canyon product, it was still salable. The coal was lignite, was useful for home heating, and had little dust. After digging those five openings and searching three seams of coal, only the last seam (slope no. 2, vein no. 3) ever produced anything of value. The seam was about 6 feet thick. The opening to this seam was 170 feet from the Rocky Ridge landing, about 72 feet above lake level. The coal was brought out of the earth on small railcars and dumped down a chute to the lakeside bunker, then taken by barge to the northwest end of Lake Whatcom and thereafter to Bellingham Bay. However, this mine was never profitable, and it closed soon after its beginning.

Today, the location of the Rocky Ridge Coal Mine is at about the 2500 block of Lake Whatcom Boulevard or the 2600 block of Woodcliff Lane. No clearly visible remnants of the mine still exist.

South Bay Coal Mine

Another mine was located at the south end of Lake Whatcom, near South Bay. It sat between what was later the Wildwood Resort and Millett's Nursery. On the side of Lookout Mountain, it was directly opposite the Blue Canyon Mine on the other side of Lake Whatcom. Its history is obscure, but it was owned by the Occidental Development Company. Like many other mines around the lake, it was never commercially productive.

Dellesta Coal Mine

A coal seam was discovered at Long Point, now called Dellesta Point, terminating at the end of Dellesta Drive.* While the quality of the bituminous coal found there was good, and the seam was reported to be twenty feet thick, the quantity of coal was small.

This coal seam was likely the same as the one described as having been discovered on February 22, 1884, on the Lanktree property.

This site likewise never produced commercial workings.

Woodlawn Coal Mine

Another coal deposit site was discovered at Woodlawn, just to the east of Long Point, slightly southeast of Agate Bay. Joseph F. Buchanan was in charge of the development of this mine, which began on October 6, 1893. Buchanan's workers drove a tunnel into the hill, chasing a seam of coal that was only two and a half feet thick. This site, too, had limited quantities of coal and never became commercially viable.

---

* SE ¼ SW ¼, Section 25, Township 38 N, Range 3 E.

Whatcom Creek Coal Mine

Yet another coal claim was filed for an area about a third of a mile below Whatcom Falls.* The coal found there was in a seam only six to sixteen inches thick, with a small area three feet thick. While its quality was good, the only coal removed was used locally, and the claim never resulted in commercial activity.

Silver Beach Coal Mine

A vein of coal was discovered at the site of the Silver Beach Hotel by Michael Pulute on November 7, 1890, as he was digging a terrace for the hotel itself. The vein was only eight feet wide. The owner of the property said he would have it analyzed and pursue the findings, as appropriate. However, the development of the hotel took precedence, and the coal was almost forgotten.

Much later, the Silver Beach Coal Mine occupied and completed the last days of the Silver Beach Hotel, as the hotel deteriorated and was about to be demolished but was resurrected as living quarters for the miners. Prospectors rediscovered coal almost directly under the hotel itself, just as the hotel was foundering with severe financial difficulties. There were five separate small veins of coal, and hopes were high that the mine would be profitable. Initial reports suggested that one vein of coal was eight to nine feet thick. Digging started in December 1921, with Otho Williams in charge of the mining, under the direction of the Pacific Atomized Fuel (or Coal) Company. In January 1922, the *Seattle Daily Times* reported that two shifts of men were digging under the Silver Beach Hotel, hoping that the mine would soon become profitable. Some of the coal discovered was called "burnt coal," but that term is not common parlance, even among geologists. If the coal had previously burned, one would expect the surrounding material to have been altered or scorched, but it was not. The precise meaning of this description remains unknown.

The mine† contained those five thin seams of coal, only one of which was even consistently 22 inches thick. The first inclined shaft was 226 feet deep, followed by a 134-foot horizontal tunnel. Further extension of the main

---

* SW ¼ NE ¼ NW ¼, Section 28, Township 38 N, Range 3 E.
† NE ¼ SW ¼, Section 22, Township 38 N, Range 3 E.

shaft tunnel to 360 feet failed to locate any commercial grade or quantity of coal. The seam being worked was 22 inches thick, far too thin for a profitable mine. One 4.5-foot-thick seam was uncovered, but it was limited in its extent, and the quality was rather poor. Those initial reports of an 8- to 9-foot-thick vein were incorrect.

By March 10, 1922, miners had reported reaching the five-hundred-foot level, and the developers expected to begin mining and delivering coal soon. There were about twenty miners employed at the Silver Beach mine at that time.

During this exploration for coal, the Silver Beach Hotel itself served as a dormitory for the miners, about fifty of them, who were digging directly under the hotel. The first floor of the previously elegant hotel, decorated inside with expensive redwood, became the dining hall and shower rooms. The men slept in the upper two floors. The actual entrance to the mine shaft was located at the site where the old roller coaster had stood. The merry-go-round building became the blacksmith's shop; the ice cream store held mining equipment.

When the search for marketable coal there was abandoned in about 1924, the hotel closed and became a derelict structure. It had been deeded (sold at a reduced price) to Ethel Henika in 1917, allegedly as partial payment for some bad White City debts, and she contracted with B.A. Campbell in January 1930 to have it demolished.

Manley Coal Mines or Manley's Camp

Manley's Camp was also called Manley's Coal Mines or Manning's Camp. Its bunkers were inconsistently described in government documents as being located at one of five different sites. However, the most reliable maps from 1923 showed Manley's Camp between the Geneva and the Rocky Ridge Coal Mines.[*]

Coal was delivered from this mine at the southeastern corner of the section to a skid road that led to its bunkers. Other small mines existed to the west of this opening. However, the Manley Coal Mine was never productive enough for commercial use.

---

[*] NW ¼, Section 1, Township 37 North, Range 3 East.

Other Coal Mines

Many other coal discoveries were reported in the 1880s and 1890s. The enthusiasm for discovering and developing coal deposits was fueled by the successes of the larger mines in the Bellingham area. It is difficult today to identify even the location of some of these discoveries because newspapers reported, with great fanfare, the alleged deposits only in vague terms: for example, "T.J. Smith's claim," which today is an obscure reference. Furthermore, it often seemed that a coal deposit was touted only as a mechanism of generating investment dollars.

Chapter 10

TIMBER, LUMBER AND SHINGLES

When Captain George Vancouver ventured into the Strait of Juan de Fuca in his sloop of war *Discovery* in 1792, he proclaimed, "The country now before us presented a most luxuriant landscape.…The whole had the appearance of a continued forest extending as far as the eye could reach."[*] He was looking at a vast collection of mostly Douglas fir, soon to become a source of great riches to the men who conquered the region and began to harvest these trees.

The first sawmill in the Bellingham Bay region was the one founded in 1853 by Captain Henry Roeder, located where Whatcom Creek emptied into Bellingham Bay. The area around this sawmill would soon become the quadruple-city complex of Whatcom, Sehome, Bellingham and Fairhaven. The lumber business would undergo wild fluctuations in economic prosperity, but the lumber barons near Bellingham who were able to withstand the rise and fall of prices would eventually become rich.

The timber industry around Lake Whatcom was well underway by the 1890s. By 1892, many small logging companies had been formed. The *Daily Reveille* in 1892–93 listed four that were under operation, ranging from fifteen to twenty employees and using five yoke cattle each.

Additional logging operations began to appear rapidly. The original lumbering industry was located on timberland near the south portion of Lake Whatcom, and independent loggers often contracted with landowners

---

[*] Blumenthal, *Early Exploration*, 107.

Lake Whatcom Lumber Company donkey engine. *Jeffcott Papers, #0334, CPNWS.*

to harvest their trees. Operations were rather small, often employing "donkey engines" for power.

Transportation of lumber to sawmills and, ultimately, to market had always been a dilemma. Lumber was heavy and bulky, and the manner of transport available often determined the success or failure of a logging enterprise. Railroads were expensive to construct and maintain because rails had to be placed in obscure and relatively inaccessible locations within the dense forests. Flumes were either natural or artificial channels of creeks or rivers that could be used to float logs downstream to the railroad spurs and then on the rails to the lake. The slope of the land next to the lake made it possible to use these chutes to deliver the smaller logs to the railroad spurs, or loggers could tow trees with steam power ("donkey engines"). The immense size of the old-growth trees around Lake Whatcom, and the large volume of water needed in the flumes for even medium-sized trees, made this method of transport largely impractical for moving the massive old-growth trees. Donkey engines and rail were often the only options. Once at lakeside, the timber would be gathered into log booms to be pulled by steamboats on Lake Whatcom to the mills at the north end of the lake. By May 1895, logging was so active that additional log boom runs (towed by the steamer *Ella*) were needed at night to accommodate the volume. These logs were brought to the Silver Beach area, where they were loaded on railcars to be carried to Bellingham Bay. Taking raw logs to Bellingham Bay required but a simple modification of the Bloedel-Donovan-Larson coal transportation system. After completion of the rail system entirely around the lake, log booms were used much less often.

The Bloedel-Donovan-Larson team recognized early that the coal business might not become as lucrative as they had wanted. The other immediate resource was timber, and it was plentiful all around the lake, as well as elsewhere. They began their association in the lumber business on August 11, 1898, as the Lake Whatcom Logging Company. Larson would ultimately become the chief investor, with Bloedel and Donovan as the businessman and director of logistics, respectively. Initially, the company was formed with an investment of $6,000: each of the three men contributed a $2,000 share.

Logging generally began at the south end of the lake and moved northward. Their first lumbering outpost was dubbed Camp One, located at South Bay (near the current location of Wildwood Resort). The Lake Whatcom Logging Company bought 3,600 acres of timber in November 1899 for $50,000, with some additional financing from investors in San Francisco. This purchase was estimated to contain 120 million feet of logs. Other small lumbering operations also sprang up around the lake, requiring the construction, often temporary, of those short railroad spurs connecting the logging to the more extensive railroad lines that delivered the product to lumbering mills in Bellingham Bay (or, later, to the Bloedel-Donovan-Larson Mills at the north end of Lake Whatcom). Larson provided the funds to buy land and lumber rights around the lake, and he also financed the railroad spurs necessary to transport the logs ever-increasing distances to Lake Whatcom's shoreline. The BB&E Railroad was extended southwest from Park to access logging camps there. Development of the railroad line completely around Lake Whatcom meant that logs had to be loaded on railcars only once. Bloedel, Donovan and Larson bought even more timberland south of the lake in the areas now known as Park, Wickersham and Alger, and they would soon expand their operations, even as far away as British Columbia.

Early lumbering ventures included the production of shingles. One of the first producers was Bartlett's Sawmill, founded on June 17, 1887, and destroyed by fire on September 2 the same year. By 1896, three companies dominated shingle production around Lake Whatcom: Thompsons, Cooks and Hodges and Jerns. By 1905, there were at least nine shingle producers around the lake, each employing 9 to 126 men. Shingle mills were abundant around the entire lake, especially at the north end. By 1905, these shingle manufacturers employed a total of over 250 men.

SHINGLE PRODUCERS

NAME	NUMBER OF SHINGLES PER DAY	NUMBER OF EMPLOYEES
Lake Shingle Company	55,000	9
Hastings Shingle Company	130,000	20
Silver Beach Shingle Company	150,000	27
Upright Shingle Company	50,000	11
Bloedel-Donovan	500,000*	?
Nicholas Jerns Sawmill Company–Silver Beach	75,000	12
Alger Shingle Company	50,000	10
Nicholas Jerns Sawmill Company–Geneva	25,000	9
Crawford Brothers Sawmill	100,000	20

*By 1915.
Numerous other shingle companies were located in Everson, Goshen, Nooksack, Maple Falls, Deming, Ferndale, Custer, Lynden, Rome, Acme, Wickersham and all of Bellingham.

By 1900, some estimates put the lumber potential around Lake Whatcom alone at 500 million to 1 billion board feet, 25 percent cedar and 75 percent fir. Bloedel-Donovan-Larson quickly realized that more profit could be had by processing the timber, rather than simply selling the raw materials. Cut lumber brought a much higher price than logs, and the manufacture of shingles, boxes, doors, sashes and other finished products soon was a part of the output of the timber business around Lake Whatcom. The Larson Lumber Company was the next step in the development of the Bloedel-Donovan-Larson enterprise. The Larson Mill was begun with its own sawmills on Lake Whatcom on July 5, 1901. This investment began with $30,000 of capital, again with the three men making equal contributions of $10,000 each. They purchased a plot of land on the northwest corner of Lake Whatcom, just south of the new town of Silver Beach. This property would soon host two major sawmills, and decades later, 12.5 acres of it

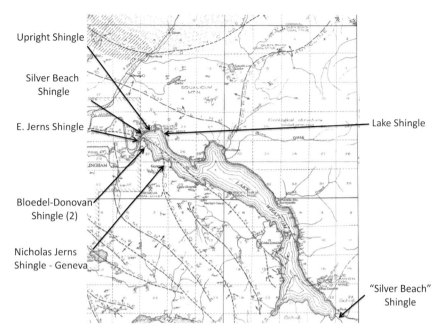

Upright Shingle

Silver Beach Shingle

E. Jerns Shingle

Lake Shingle

Bloedel-Donovan Shingle (2)

Nicholas Jerns Shingle - Geneva

"Silver Beach" Shingle

Location of shingle mills immediately around the perimeter of Lake Whatcom. The "Silver Beach" Shingle Mill at the south end of the lake operated only from 1904 to 1908, and it was not actually located at Silver Beach. *Adapted from plate no. 1, Olaf P. Jenkins,* Geological Investigation of the Coal Fields of Western Whatcom County, Washington, *State of Washington Division of Geology, Bulletin No. 28, Olympia, WA, 1923, Department of Conservation, State of Washington.*

would become Bloedel-Donovan Park. The first mill began operation in 1901, the second in 1906. In 1903, the first Bloedel-Donovan-Larson mill processed 25 million board feet of lumber and 75 million shingles. By January 25, 1904, the capacity of this complex would be 100,000 board feet of lumber and 30,000 shingles per day. It was a huge operation, employing 140 workers and paying $125,000 in salaries during the year. The two mills were estimated to be worth $500,000, while the entire assets of the company exceeded $2,000,000.

Counting other logging companies, as many as 525 men were employed in this industry in the early 1900s, with a payroll of over $1,500 per day. The output was estimated to be about 800,000 feet of lumber per day. That year there were twelve major logging camps, the largest being the Lake Whatcom Logging Company.

By 1907, the Larson Mill dominated lumber production in the area. Mill A of the company had opened on July 25, 1901, and even in that early year, the output was 100,000 feet of lumber per every 10-hour shift. The Larson

Log at the entrance to the Bloedel-Donovan Lumber Mills, 1913. In earlier years, the sign said, "Larson Lumber Company." This tree was 12 feet in diameter, 275 feet high, contained 105,000 board feet of lumber and was about 700 years old. *Biery Papers, #3191, CPNWS.*

shingle mills had acquired other mills in the area, and their combined output was 715,000 shingles per day. The lumber business was so lucrative that the Larson Mill began an expansion in December 1906, dubbed Mill B, capable of adding 165,000 feet of lumber processed per 10-hour shift. Both Mill A and Mill B working simultaneously could produce 265,000 feet, or over 500,000 feet daily, if the owners chose to run a double shift. Additionally, over 90 percent of the lumber was finished with a smooth surface, or planed.

Equipment was state-of-the-art. A 130-foot smokestack towered over the entire complex, which included a "monster gangsaw" anchored into a 250-ton concrete base. A "horizontal resaw" machine had wheels 11

Bloedel-Donovan Lumber Mills, 1925. Workers' homes are on the lower left. *Whatcom Museum, 1980.0074.000603.*

Dock near Silver Beach at Bloedel-Donovan Mills. Note that both lumber and coal were being delivered here at this time. The location is just south of today's boat launch in Bloedel-Donovan Park. The steamer at the right is the *Ella. Whatcom Museum, 2010.0055.000173.*

feet in diameter. It was a bandsaw with a blade 16 inches wide and 65 feet long (one of only three such machines on the entire West Coast). A 750-horsepower Allis-Chalmers steam engine drove the large saws, its 14-foot flywheel dwarfing the men who worked it; they were protected from accidental injury by its concrete enclosure. The mill itself employed 267 men, not counting the 225 loggers who supplied the tree trunks; in total, the Larson Mill employed over 600 people, the largest payroll north of Seattle. Corporately, the Larson Lumber Mill was separate from the Lake Whatcom Logging Company, though the officers and owners of both companies were the same. The latter business owned 27,000 acres of red cedar (shingles) and fir (lumber). The logging part of the company had 14 "donkey engines" for the felling and movement of the trees. It owned 21 miles of railway tracks and three locomotive engines, connecting to the Northern Pacific and the Great Northern lines.

LAKE WHATCOM SAWMILLS AND SHINGLE MILLS

COMPANY NAME	LOCATION	DATES OF OPERATION	OWNERS	COMMENTS
Barker Logging Company	Lake Whatcom	1920–27	S.W. Barker	
Bartlett and Son Sawmill	Lake Whatcom	1887	Bartlett	Opened on June 17; burned in October
Bloedel-Donovan Lumber Mills–Sawmill	Larson	1913–46	Julius H. Bloedel; John J. Donovan; Peter Larson	Became Columbia Valley Lumber Company
Bloedel-Donovan Lumber Mills	Park	1910	Julius H. Bloedel; John J. Donovan; Peter Larson	
Byles, Lee N.	Park	1912	Lee N. Byles	

Company Name	Location	Dates of Operation	Owners	Comments
Columbia Valley Lumber Company	Larson	1911–62	Julius H. Bloedel; John J. Donovan; Ralph A. Clark	Purchased Bloedel-Donovan Lumber Mill in 1946
Columbia Valley Lumber Company Sawmill	Lake Whatcom	1949		
Cook Shingle Mill	Lake Whatcom	1895	J.A. Cook	
Empire Cedar Company Shingle Mill No. 1	Lake Whatcom	1894		
Guthrie and Manning Logging	Lake Whatcom	1890s	Guthrie, Manning	
Hanner Logging Company	Park	1926	Hanner	
Hanner Shingle Mill	Park	1926	Hanner	Elsewhere spelled Haner
Hastings Shingle Manufacturing Company	Silver Beach	1901–06	James McNair, President	Burned in 1903; sold to Larson Lumber Company in 1906; burned in 1909
Nicholas Jerns Shingle Mill	Silver Beach	1898–1925	Nicholas Jerns	
Lake Whatcom Logging Company	Blue Canyon	1890		

COMPANY NAME	LOCATION	DATES OF OPERATION	OWNERS	COMMENTS
Lake Whatcom Logging Company	Silver Beach	1890–1913	Julius H. Bloedel; John J. Donovan; Peter Larson	Became Bloedel-Donovan Lumber Mills
Lake Whatcom Shingle Company	Lake Whatcom	1899	H.O. Hughey	Also called Lake Shingle Company
Larson Lumber Company–Sawmill	Silver Beach	1890–1913	Julius H. Bloedel; John J. Donovan; Peter Larson	Became Bloedel-Donovan Lumber Mills
J.A. McCormick	Park	1912	J.A. McCormick	
McDonald Brothers Logging	Blue Canyon	1890	McDonald; McDonald	
Mogul Logging Company	Lake Whatcom	1904–11	Lee N. Byles; George Nolte; Charles F. Nolte	Located at north end of Lake Whatcom
Port Hadlock Mill Company	Lake Whatcom	1900		
Silver Beach Shingle Company*	Silver Beach	1902–10	N.O. Hughley; J.D. Rockey	Sold to Upright Shingle Company in 1910
Stinson and Park	Lake Whatcom	1886–89	Thomas D. Stinson; Hugh Park	
Thompson and Company	Lake Whatcom	1894	Thompson	

Company name	Location	Dates of operation	Owners	Comments
Underwood Shingle Company	Lake Whatcom	1895	F.G. Underwood	
Upright Shingle Company Shingle Mill	Silver Beach	1902–03	James L. Gilfilen; R.F. Gilfilen	
L.R. Waite	Park	1912	L.R. Waite	
Washington Mill Company	Lake Whatcom	1899–1900		
Wood-Knight Logging Company	Park	1928	E.K. Wood; A.W. Knight	
Young Brothers Mill	Lake Whatcom	1895	Young; Young	

*Note: Another Silver Beach Shingle Company operated from 1904 to 1908, located at the south end of Lake Whatcom along Anderson Creek, and two other Silver Beach Shingle companies operated in the Geneva area in the 1914–16 era (Sections 6 and 26, Township 37 North, Range 4 East).

Other shingle mills that were not counted in this listing were a bit farther from Lake Whatcom: Miller's Sawmill and the Lars Peterson Mill.

Fires were a common hazard for all mills. The Hastings Shingle Mill in Silver Beach burned on May 9, 1903, when the dry kiln and loading shed caught fire, destroying four million shingles, estimated to be worth $10,000.

E.K. Wood Lumber owned much of the timber on the east side of Lake Whatcom, and it had large plots on the west side, as well.

Owners and officers of these companies changed frequently.

By this time, the Bloedel-Donovan-Larson enterprise had established a company town, though one far more complex and widespread than the usual mining or logging village. It had over thirty-five cottages, parks, stores, gardens and even a school and a church. The businessmen allowed and encouraged employees to settle on land where only lumber slashings remained, and they sold property to employees for homes at greatly reduced prices, disposing of over thirty thousand acres in this way. The Bloedel-Donovan business was far ahead of its time in many respects.

Bloedel-Donovan picnic, September 10, 1896. *Biery Papers, #2524, CPNWS.*

The company was very good to its employees. Yearly, it held grand parties and picnics to thank the workers for their hard work and production. It was common for the Bloedel and Donovan families to host smaller gatherings to show residents of Bellingham and their employees' families the operation of the business. Photos from the time depicted anachronistic images of women in fancy dresses inspecting the donkey engines and the huge sawblades at the timber mills. Bloedel, Donovan and Larson indeed seemed to be benevolent landlords.

In 1913, the Lake Whatcom Logging Company, the Larson Lumber Mill, the Bellingham Bay Lumber Mill (also called the Cornwall Mill) and the Larson Cargo Mill downtown combined to become the Bloedel-Donovan Lumber Mill, whose main lumbering facility was located on what is now Electric Avenue in Silver Beach. Its offices would eventually be located at the waterfront on Bellingham Bay at the foot of Cornwall Avenue, in a building that still stands. The Bloedel-Donovan-Larson timber franchise would become one of the largest lumber manufacturers on the West Coast; in 1928, it was the largest sawmill in the world, with the majority of the milling being done in Bellingham Bay at the Cargo Mill. Utilizing all grades of lumber, the Bloedel-Donovan enterprise built a box factory in Bellingham Bay in 1918, opposite its offices.

Aerial view of the Bloedel-Donovan Lumber Mill on Lake Whatcom, undated. *Biery Papers, #1958, CPNWS.*

Aerial view of Bloedel-Donovan Park site and a portion of the remnants of the Bloedel-Donovan Lumber Mill, September 2, 1947. Note that today's park was mostly unused land. *Whatcom Museum, 1995.0001.000006.*

Aerial view of Bloedel-Donovan Park in 2022 with mill structures superimposed. *Adapted from CityIQ Map, City of Bellingham.*

A 2023 aerial photo of Bloedel-Donovan Park and site of prior lumber mills, looking south-southeast. Today's Old Mill Village sits where Mill B was located. The remnants of the old wharf can be seen as deteriorating pilings projecting above the waterline. Most of the lumber mill structures had been located to the south of the wharf. *Photo courtesy of Matthew Greene.*

The timber immediately around Lake Whatcom was plentiful, but the supply close to the lake was quickly exhausted, even as early as 1895. Logging camps had moved farther and farther from the shores by the early 1900s. By 1918, almost all the first-growth timber around the lake had been felled. However, loggers still towed their product to the edge of the lake and floated it to the mills at the northern end of Lake Whatcom. Many small and temporary railroad spurs still connected lumbering sites to the edge of the lake.

Lumbering peaked in the 1920s, at which time over thirty-one different sawmills were operating around Lake Whatcom. As logging began to decline, Lumber Mill No. 1 (Mill A, the northernmost one) was the first to be leveled, following the closure of the Bloedel-Donovan Mills in 1945. In September 1946, Julius and Mina Bloedel donated the tract of 12.5 acres to become a city park, along with $150,000 to develop the property. They stipulated that the land was to be developed solely for a park for the city of Bellingham and that it was to be called Bloedel-Donovan Park in perpetuity. The Bloedels set a goal of August 11, 1948, as the date of the park's dedication, which would coincide with the fiftieth anniversary of the incorporation of Lake Whatcom Logging Company. They achieved their goal, and the park was dedicated on that day. Mill B continued its operation as part of the Columbia Valley Lumber Company until it burned on January 16, 1958. The planing portion of the mill continued under the Robinson Plywood and Lumber Company until the mid-1960s.

Chapter 11

SETTLEMENTS AND TOWNS

Silver Beach

The history of the town of Silver Beach cannot be separated from the history of the Silver Beach Hotel or from that of the White City Amusement Park. All developed at approximately the same time, and even the management and finances of the three overlapped.

The Silver Beach area around the north end of Lake Whatcom was nothing but timberland in the mid-1800s. As settlers came to the region, Silver Beach (not yet called by that name) was home to the hardy and the common. There were no rich or elite to be found. But as the local population grew, investors saw potential for land speculation, development, housing and recreation, as well as logging and mining. The unincorporated land would soon give way to a platted city, which was incorporated and, finally, included within the city limits of Bellingham.

The first owner of the land to become Silver Beach was James P. DeMattos. He was a lawyer who would become a Bellingham mayor many times over. He acquired government land that would be repeatedly sold over the space of only a few months.[*] (Considering the wild land speculation underway at the time, it was common for a piece of property to change hands multiple times in a week, and some were even sold more than once on the same day.) DeMattos sold his land to Philip E. and Susanna Dickinson on

---

[*] Lots No. 4 and No. 5, NE ¼ SW ¼, Section 22, Township 38 N, Range 3 E.

Plat map of Silver Beach, 1890. *Whatcom County Tax Parcel Viewer.*

June 7, 1888, apparently even before DeMattos received his final land patent. The Dickinsons sold this property to Edward F.G. Carlyon for $7,500 on February 19, 1890. That year, Carlyon was busy acquiring land, buildings and even boats used in and around what would become Silver Beach, a name chosen by Mary A. Hummel, a local landowner. Carlyon purchased a boathouse and boats from Louis Belanger on June 17, 1890. These would become the docks below the Silver Beach Hotel.

E.F.G. Carlyon had purchased the three hundred acres (lots no. 4 and no. 5) for what was to be a resort on the north end of Lake Whatcom. The Silver Beach Hotel would be an integral part of his entire project. The Allerton and McFarland Company, civil engineers in Fairhaven, surveyed the proposed town of Silver Beach, the plat being drawn in April 1890 and filed on May 23, 1890, with the best site reserved for the hotel. Technically, Carlyon established the town, with Jones as his attorney. Carlyon preserved for himself the rights to mine for coal and bore for oil on the entire three hundred acres.

Development proceeded rapidly. Telephones became operational on June 17, 1890. The Silver Beach Saloon had Joe Mattas as its early proprietor. Two restaurants soon appeared. The Silver Beach school opened on October 20, 1890, with twelve pupils. The post office opened on August 21, 1890, with Samuel Forteath as the postmaster.

Jones and Carlyon found themselves busy platting the town, arranging for improvement of the roads, building a plank highway from New Whatcom to Silver Beach, constructing the Silver Beach Hotel, procuring trolley service to the area and encouraging boat traffic to the area from everywhere on Lake Whatcom.

The wooden plank road itself was quite an impressive project, running from New Whatcom to Silver Beach. It was completed in the summer of 1890. Civic-minded citizens (as well as those who wanted to see their land appreciate in value) contributed to its construction. In May 1890, Mary Hummel donated $500 to the cause. Local residents insisted that travel on the roads to Silver Beach be pleasant. When businessmen began to nail advertising boards on trees along the route, local officials removed them, stating that they wanted to keep the drive beautiful without being polluted with advertising signs.

An unexpected downside of such construction was the increase in frequency of fires on the road itself caused by discarded cigars and cigarettes. Furthermore, transport of heavy items damaged the road itself. When the steamship *Edith* was pulled along the wooden street to Lake Whatcom, the damage to the planks was extensive.

Jones and Carlyon began sales of lots by advertising eighty plots of land for twenty-seven dollars per acre. Like most good entrepreneurs, Jones and Carlyon printed a monthly pamphlet, using the presses of the *Sehome Gazette*, touting the benefits of this new venture and listing the lots remaining for sale.

In the years 1889–90, Jones and Carlyon were exceedingly busy with multiple projects, beyond just developing, platting and promoting Silver Beach. Their principal business was Jones and Carlyon Real Estate, located at Holly and Elk in Sehome (now Holly and State Street) and at Fourteenth Street and McKenzie Avenue in Fairhaven. Furthermore, they sold both life and fire insurance. Jones and Carlyon had built the Grand Central Hotel at Forest and Holly Streets. Simultaneously, they promoted the Alabama Street Addition to New Whatcom, as well as plans for building the Silver Beach Hotel and Pavilion (first named the Caledonian Hotel, though the name never took hold). Because of all this activity, Jones and Carlyon defaulted

Ad for Silver Beach, June 4, 1890. Sehome Morning Gazette, *CP.NWS*.

on some of their debts in December 1890. Selling assets to satisfy their creditors, they avoided officially declaring bankruptcy, but their partnership would ultimately dissolve.

The construction of the Silver Beach Hotel was in large part the result of the real estate ventures of Edward Carlyon. Reginald Jones and Carlyon, both Bellingham lawyers and real estate brokers, started the Silver Beach Land Company in 1889, with their major project being the construction of the Silver Beach Hotel. Elegant and finished in redwood, it opened officially on May 30, 1891. It was both charming and first-class. The *Bellingham Bay Express* on August 12, 1890, reported that it "would be a credit to a city of 10,000 people. Neat and pretty design and admirably arranged for convenience and comfort, it will be one of the most popular resorts on the Sound, as the surroundings have every attraction for the tourist in search of sport, recreation, and health." The hotel boasted a large dining room with exquisite food. Jones, attempting to promote business for the hotel, held a grand banquet for newspaper writers on September 3, 1891, with the goal of inducing favorable publicity for the hotel. Samuel Forteath was the

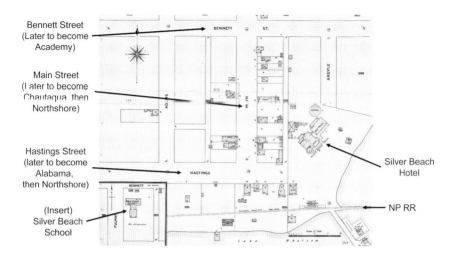

Bennett Street (Later to become Academy)

Main Street (Later to become Chautaqua, then Northshore)

Hastings Street (later to become Alabama, then Northshore)

(Insert) Silver Beach School

Silver Beach Hotel

NP RR

Map of Silver Beach, 1904, showing the location of the Silver Beach Hotel. "NP RR" = Northern Pacific Railroad. *Sanborn Maps, 1904, CPNWS.*

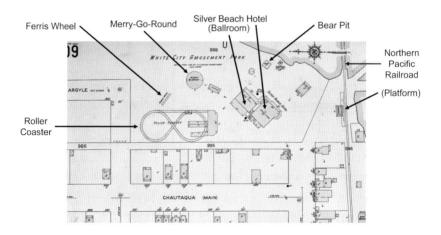

Ferris Wheel

Merry-Go-Round

Silver Beach Hotel (Ballroom)

Bear Pit

Northern Pacific Railroad

(Platform)

Roller Coaster

Silver Beach, 1913. Note that a fence and a row of houses separate the park from Main Street (Chautaqua Street), and the trolley is not illustrated. Map is reoriented with north to the left. (Note also that the street is spelled Chautaqua, while the organization is spelled Chautauqua.) *Sanborn Maps, 1913, CPNWS.*

original proprietor, and he was also the postmaster of the Silver Beach Post Office. There were fifteen or sixteen bedrooms. Each suite cost three dollars per day, with a discount for those who resided there longer than a week. At first, guests came to the hotel by the Silver Beach Hotel Stage, driven from downtown Bellingham at the corner of Elk (now State Street) and Holly by George Geer. He made the round trip three times daily for a fare of twenty-five cents one way. But on February 18, 1892, the streetcar trolley on the Fairhaven and New Whatcom Railway initiated service on the Lake Line from downtown Bellingham, making the trip in mere minutes. Furthermore, the fare for the trolley was only ten cents one way. Geer's stage immediately disappeared. For those wanting to provide their own transportation in the early days of the hotel, it provided a stable for visiting horses.

Boat racing was part of the activity around Lake Whatcom, and it was a lively scene around the hotel. Races were held on Sundays in the summer, and they drew hundreds of guests to the hotel and the surrounding environs.

Early managers of the hotel included both Jones and Carlyon, though the investors soon employed J.L. Thatcher as the manager, who also tended the bar and the hotel's phone. In 1892, the hotel was briefly leased to J.L. Thatcher and Warren Burgess of New Whatcom, who reopen it on April 1, 1892. The investors' dream of further developing the area as a resort community was dashed with the economic crash that began in May 1893. The New York stock market crash affected places as far away as the Pacific Northwest. Thatcher departed and became a rancher; the Fairhaven and New Whatcom Electric Railway also briefly folded.

One major draw for the Silver Beach locale was the availability of liquor, though officially, it was not legal. Alcohol was not sold in Bellingham during the early 1890s. Many traveled to Silver Beach and its hotel for their beer, wine and liquor. The Lynden *Pioneer Press*, in May 1890, reported that Lauchlin McKenzie had applied to the city for a liquor license "for the town of Silver Beach" and was rejected. Thereafter, Samuel Forteath applied for a liquor license in February 1892, but the Whatcom County Commissioners also rejected his application because the legal codes prohibited selling alcohol within one mile of a city. Nevertheless, trying to keep the hotel afloat financially, the owners continued to promote their alcohol sales, and the clientele thereafter became a bit less reputable. The irony of the hotel's business model was that, while promoting alcohol, they would soon open a business combatting alcoholism.

Not all was well between Jones and Carylon. In July 1891, they had a falling-out, and they initiated lawsuits against each other. Jones sued Carlyon

Pier on Lake Whatcom, circa 1890–1900. Photo is taken looking south from approximately the BB&E (later the Northern Pacific) railroad track, just below the Silver Beach Hotel. The steamer partially obscured is said to be the *Cora Blake*. *Whatcom Museum, 1996.0010.007106.*

and John E. Baker. Jones claimed that the Carlyon/Baker enterprise was acting against the interests of Jones's clients. A judge ruled in favor of Carlyon/Baker, stating that an arbitrator had to intervene on the matter of the Carlyon/Jones partnership. Eventually Carlyon and Jones split; later, they would declare bankruptcy.

Many struggling businesses partner with organizations that might complement their revenue. The Silver Beach Hotel did exactly that in 1893. George O. Smith, manager of the Panter Institute for the Cure of the Liquor, Opium and Tobacco Habits in New Whatcom, opened a sanitorium at the Silver Beach Hotel on June 8, 1893. The Panter Improved Remedy Company used bichloride of gold infusions to combat alcoholism, drug addiction (opium, morphine, cocaine, tobacco) and other maladies. Smith was the clinic's director, hawking Panter's Improved Remedy, a purported treatment for addiction. This treatment would become even more popular elsewhere at the turn of the 1900s, as it cited the Cook Remedy as its predecessor, claiming it had treated over twenty-two thousand patients successfully. The *Fairhaven Herald*'s coverage of Smith declared, "Observation and experience prove that all who habitually indulge in these terrible habits become bestial, and are, as soon as the appetite becomes stronger than the power of the will, made slaves bound with threads or hawsers until it becomes a mighty mesh of steel which no victim unaided can break. A panacea is now offered." The cure also promised to relieve "sore throat, eruptions on your body, falling hair, swollen glands, pains in the bones, or severe continued headaches," as well as "blood poison." Smith's physician accomplice administered treatment at the Silver Beach Hotel, where "patients or public receive good accommodation at the hotel at reasonable charges." His cure was touted to be "safe, sure and painless."

Panter's Improved Remedy was a corporation registered in Washington State. The articles of incorporation stated that an "Institute" would be formally opened on June 5, 1893, at the Silver Beach Hotel. They claimed that Dr. Panter of Omaha himself would be present for the grand opening.

This treatment had been being evaluated elsewhere by the Women's Temperance Alliance, as early as 1891, seeking evidence for its effectiveness. Bichloride of gold treatments were injections given up to four times daily for a few days, up to a week. After treatment, the patient who ingested any alcohol would become violently ill (much like disulfiram of more recent decades). This reaction would lead to the abolition of any desire for drugs or alcohol. However, after these treatments became popularized, an occasional patient receiving the therapy would abruptly die, causing some pause in the enthusiasm for the infusions. Lawsuits were filed in various states, and the expected rush to book rooms at the Silver Beach Hotel never materialized. The treatment's uncertain efficacy and adverse effects deterred the masses from coming. Even retrofitting the Silver Beach Hotel facility with its new paint and wallpaper proved unprofitable, as few opted for the treatments. The Panter Company's sanitoriums elsewhere in the United States and Canada also faltered. The arrangement between Panter and the Silver Beach Hotel lasted only one year. The Panter Remedy Company of Chicago would continue; however, the Silver Beach Hotel was not to be one of its beneficiaries.

Later, during the depression of the 1890s, the hotel continued to falter. Rarely, the entire facility would be rented by a family or families, as it was in 1895, when J.W. Morgan and George Gage, two renters, had the building completely to themselves.

On July 25, 1896, the Whatcom *Weekly Blade* reported that A. Elsterit had leased the hotel and renamed it the New World, "where all kinds of liquid fluid can be enjoyed." In 1896, almost ten years before the opening of White City, the hotel was said to have fruit stands, a shooting gallery, a merry-go-round and dancing. When the economy improved at the beginning of the twentieth century, the hotel reopened under the direction of John Greulich, a tobacconist who had a store on Elk Street and who had bought the Silver Beach Hotel for $3,000.

A dance pavilion was added to the east side of the original hotel complex in 1901, opening in May. The dance floor was large, thirty-six by sixty feet, and a porch was also constructed to provide outside walkspace and a view of the lake and mountains. Concurrent with the addition of the dance pavilion, the original fifteen to sixteen suites were converted to thirty simpler individual rooms. The owners hoped to attract a slightly less wealthy crowd, but the repurposing of the rooms had little effect on the financial viability of the hotel. The complex also had an ice cream store, named Marshall's Palace. The owners further added a few rather mundane amusements trying to attract paying customers: "flying swings" and "shoot-the-chutes" were intended to bolster profits. They didn't.

As with any destination resort, the hotel's occupancy was greatly dependent on the weather. In the summer, attendance was fine, but in the fall, winter and spring, the cool and rain made financial viability tenuous. Having alcohol and tobacco available enticed a few visitors, but the hotel itself continued to struggle.

As the hotel's clientele became seedier, local residents began to complain. In March 1903, deputy sheriff John Parberry arrested August Johnson, the barkeeper at the Silver Beach Hotel, for selling alcohol without a license. He pled not guilty. Also in 1903, the hotel again changed management; John Whalen and David Wurtenberg became managers. Wurtenberg was a beer salesman for Bellingham Bay Brewery, and he was forced out of his role at the Silver Beach Hotel soon after local residents discovered his connections.

People living in Silver Beach wanted their community to become an official entity. Efforts to incorporate were thwarted in November 1905 because county regulations required at least 300 persons to be living in the proposed city. Silver Beach, at that time, had only 270. A repeat attempt in October 1907 suffered the same fate when election officials discovered that many of the signers of the incorporation petition were not actually legal residents of the proposed town. Silver Beach was finally annexed to Bellingham in March 1908, by a vote of sixty-seven to twenty-eight. Bellingham approved the acquisition on April 14, 1908.

However, when Silver Beach residents voted to become part of the city of Bellingham, an unappreciated outcome was the continued inability to sell alcohol legally. While belonging to Bellingham had some advantages, one

Ice Cream Store | Silver Beach School | Silver Beach Hotel

Bear Cage | Bellingham Bay and Eastern RR, later Northern Pacific RR

Silver Beach seen from the east side of Lake Whatcom, approximately where the Lake Shingle Company Mill sat, date unknown. *Biery Papers, #3352, CPNWS.*

disadvantage was that liquor sales at White City and the Silver Beach Hotel needed approval from the City of Bellingham. The previous lax enforcement of dry laws came to an end. The local Woman's Christian Temperance Union prevailed; both the Silver Beach Hotel and White City, for a time, technically became dry.

On April 23, 1906, Marshall's Palace, the ice cream store and the dance hall close to the Silver Beach Hotel were destroyed by fire.

The craze for amusement parks in the late 1800s and early 1900s spawned a "White City" in many locales. The 1893 Chicago World's Fair (also called the World's Columbian Exposition) drew thousands of attendees from all over the United States, as well as the rest of the world. It had extensive entertainment venues, including the first Ferris wheel, named after its inventor, George Washington Gale Ferris Jr., who was trying to create something spectacular to compete with the Eiffel Tower in Paris from the 1889 Paris Exhibition. The Chicago World's Fair was characterized both by the white color of its many buildings and the brilliance of the new electric lights, powered by alternating current. This appearance spawned the nickname White City. This began a craze for other cities to have brilliantly illuminated parks or carnivals, each likewise called White City.

In May 1906, Clarence H. Chandler, a wealthy investor from Pittsburgh, came to Bellingham to visit his friend William Gwynn, a local real estate

Silver Beach Hotel, July 18, 1891, prior to the addition of a dance hall on its northeast. *Whatcom Museum, 1979.0057.000162.*

mogul. Chandler and Gwynn fished around Lake Whatcom, and Chandler was impressed with the beauty of the region. Furthermore, its development potential was striking. Chandler moved to the area, and the two men formed the Silver Beach Amusement Company. Chandler invested heavily in the proposed amusement park, and by the time he finished, he had sunk $100,000 into a twelve-acre facility he and Gwynn called White City, next to the Silver Beach Hotel, which they also bought. One report said that all property would be held in Gwynn's name, though later events would prove that report to be false. They changed the name of the hotel to the White City Hotel and immediately built a figure-of-eight roller coaster (designed and constructed by Charles Stauffer of Pittsburgh, a well-known architect of such devices) and a seventy-five-foot-high Ferris wheel (built by S.E. Walling, likewise a well-known builder of Ferris wheels who had brought one of his Ferris wheels to Bellingham on two or three previous occasions on a temporary basis).

The park also had a merry-go-round, another ice cream store and a boathouse and wharf for boat rentals. Even live animals were an attraction to visitors: for a while, a cage near the water's edge housed live bears. The park touted a herd of deer and a pair of bald eagles, as well. In addition, there was a large picnic area and a ball field to the northeast of the amusements. Chandler envisioned a new water system for the hotel and park. Furthermore, he dreamed of constructing an "Enchanted Castle," a "Katzenjammer House," a "Crystal Maze," a "Cave of the Winds" and many more rides: a new shoot-the-chutes, a bump-the-bumps, a scenic railway and a "laughing gallery," supposedly a room with entertainment that would cause visitors to laugh uncontrollably. As was the trend of the time, Chandler even declared that White City would have infant incubators, a novel display that defied patient confidentiality, though their use would be beneficial when needed, as exhibiting infant patients in these incubators was one of few ways to finance such an expensive medical innovation in that era.

The first opening of White City was held on the weekend of Saturday, September 29, 1906, but this was seemingly just a trial run; the real "first grand opening" was actually held on Sunday, October 7. Over three thousand people came for this event, though local newspapers described the day as "foggy and gray." Park entry was free; fees were only charged for using the rides and other facilities such as the boat rental. The Ferris wheel, merry-go-round and roller coaster were all in operation on the first day.

However, the park soon closed in October as temperatures dropped and rain descended on the region. This pattern would become part of the demise of the amusement park years later: it could only remain open from about late May to early October.

Gwynn would be the manager on-site, and Chandler was the off-site investor, spending his winters elsewhere. Chandler had plans to build even more attractions at White City: a toboggan slide, a dance pavilion on the edge of the water, a roller rink, a house of mirrors, a "tunnel of love," a baseball diamond, a penny arcade and tennis courts. Gwynn and Chandler planned an additional wharf near the hotel to supplement the county wharf. They proposed to dig a well for fresh water beyond the limitless (but perhaps dirtier) water available from Lake Whatcom. Most of these amenities actually came to pass. Additional amusements included the "flying flaming dive," a woman who would climb a tall tower in an asbestos suit, set herself on fire and dive into a pool of water. There were acrobats, tightrope walkers, "slackrope" walkers (similar to a tightrope, but made of a wider, more flexible weblike material and more difficult because the band can stretch and move) and jugglers. Chandler's dreams never stopped: he envisioned a vaudeville stage and an "electric theater." Neither of the latter two projects materialized.

Ball games and picnics were held at the adjacent park grounds, and smaller games and food and drink sales supported the party atmosphere. The Fourth of July was always well attended, and good summer weather drew large crowds. It was fashionable for locals (Ferndale, Lynden, Birch Bay, Blaine), as well as visitors from Bellingham, to find their names in the newspaper as having attended gatherings at Silver Beach or White City. Local residents also planned to build their own piers to take advantage of the lake's recreational possibilities.

The park reopened on Memorial Day in May 1907 (this was actually the "official grand opening" of White City, though its other two "grand openings" at the end of the previous summer had been well attended), and a reported ten thousand visitors attended on this Memorial Day weekend. The trolley from the Whatcom County Railway and Light was partially responsible for the success, taking only seven and a half minutes one way. This year, William H. Oldwin ran the hotel restaurant; he was experienced and well-received.

The park also boasted thousands of electric lights and a heated "natatorium," today called a swimming pool, advertised as being ready for use on June 20. Furthermore, the northern apex of Lake Whatcom had a sandy beach with a safe slope for all swimmers.

On July 4, newspapers reporting on White City claimed that nearly all of Bellingham was there. Veterans had a special day in August, with over one thousand former military servicemembers in attendance. When business was particularly good, the rails of both the trolley system and the BB&E were used, with the railroad flatcars fitted with benches added for the passengers.

Initially, the novelty of the park drew thousands, but as the newness wore off, the park's revenues decreased. Promoters hawked carnivals and special events to bolster attendance. Fleet Week was an event to honor sailors from the U.S. Navy; Airship Week brought hot air balloons and dirigibles for rides and observation. The venue was also frequently rented to local businesses, churches, civic clubs and military organizations. Summer carnivals were popular, with traveling shows augmenting the permanent attractions.

In July 1907, a massive fair was scheduled to take place at White City, touted as "the greatest carnival ever held in this part of the state." The permanent attractions were highlighted, such as the new 75-×-150-foot dance pavilion constructed over the waters of Lake Whatcom, capable of accommodating four hundred persons at one time. The wooden dance floor was unique, and a stage for the musicians was suspended above the dance floor, giving a "clear and unobstructed floor for the dancers." On July 22, visiting entertainment included "the Great Davenport, the king of high wire performers, and Lenora

Davenport, the queen of the high wire, who actually performs the most hazardous and startling feat of dashing daringly over a slender cable, 100 feet high on an ordinary safety bicycle, while Mr. Davenport does a hair-raising performance in a trapeze suspended below."* Additional advertisements touted "the only wild girl in captivity," the Georgia Jubilee Singers, a Chinese village, the Great Anderson (an artist), "Van Ronk's Moving Picture Show," gypsies and the permanent amusements of the park. Nevertheless, the event was financially unsuccessful. The promoters fell into debt, and a few were arrested for their failure to pay their debts. Other events in 1907 included a three-day veterans' encampment and a huge Labor Day celebration.

In 1908, the Great White Fleet—the U.S. naval armada—came to Bellingham. Navy sailors were honored when they arrived in Bellingham Bay, and special trolley runs transported the men from downtown to White City and back. Everything was free for sailors, including food and transportation.

In mid-August, a dirigible airship called the *America*, captained by James Moore, came to the park (August 23–29), scheduled to make two ascensions daily. This contraption was over one hundred feet long, frail and quite susceptible to the elements. It had a three-cylinder engine powering its forward, backward and lateral motion. Its direction was controlled by the pilot moving on a triangular frame, his weight acting as ballast that guided the balloon. On August 23, the crowd (estimated at seven thousand) waited many hours to see the ascension (admission twenty-five cents), but modest winds kept the airship from rising. At the end of the day, however, it rose three times, though Captain Moore would not allow passengers because of the precarious nature of its stability in the winds.

Gwynn and Chandler would remain owners; Gwynn remained the on-site manager until 1909. The park at this time was variably called the White City Amusement Park, the Silver Beach Amusement Company or simply White City.

In early January 1909, the owners of White City were accused of cruelty to the deer kept on the premises, though Chandler and Gwynn denied the charges. They claimed that the deer were well-fed and that their roaming around the neighborhood led to the incorrect conclusion that they were being neglected.

That year, Chandler took over the day-to-day management of the hotel and park complex, and he had some improvements he wished to make to the property. He desired to construct a chute-the-chutes (always a part of

---

* *Blaine Journal*, July 12, 1907; *Bellingham Herald*, July 17 and July 20, 1907.

Left: Ad for the dirigible exposition at White City from the *Bellingham Herald*, August 22, 1908. *CPNWS.*

Below: Captain James Moore's airship at White City, August 1908. *Whatcom Museum, 1973.0035.000041.*

the plans for the park), a vaudeville theater and a beer garden. This latter proposal for the sale of alcohol again met stiff resistance from Silver Beach residents, and local sensitivities prohibited its implementation. These were the years of temperance societies, and they objected to such decadent behavior. The Temperance unions prevailed. Chandler was again denied a permit to serve alcohol on the premises of White City or in the hotel.

In July 1909, the White City Amusement Company was formally incorporated and sold publicly, with Chandler and Gwynn as incorporators. It proposed selling three thousand shares of stock for a total of $75,000.

The first Chautauqua was held at White City in 1910. The Chautauqua movement was a cultural, educational and social enterprise that originated in Chautauqua, New York, in 1874. Both the organization and the events themselves were called "Chautauqua" or "Chautauquas." By 1925, there were at least thirty-three Chautauqua organizations in the state of Washington alone. These organizations promoted literature, music, dance, culture, theater, drama and education in general.

A smaller two-story hotel on Main Street—the first hotel in the area (not the Silver Beach Hotel), built by Carlyon and Jones and then owned in 1910 by Olaf Glad, facing Main Street (Chautaqua Street)—burned to the ground on March 27. Only the efforts of a volunteer fire bucket brigade kept the roller coaster from burning, as well.

Chandler, who had taken over as manager in 1909, had a stroke (the term was *apoplexy* in the early 1900s) on May 26, 1910, and died. Initially, it appeared that Chandler, a widower, had left no will, but he was a legal resident of Charleroi, Washington County, Pennsylvania. Inquiries there produced a will that left the entirety of Chandler's estate to his daughter Genevieve W. "Vera" Chandler Phipps of Denver, except for $2,000 that Chandler gave to a business assistant. Chandler's estate was estimated by some to be worth about $75,000; he had been the major owner of the Silver Beach property. Phipps was also named as the executrix of his last will and testament. Phipps inherited Chandler's portion of the Silver Beach Park and the White City Resort; however, she was wealthy and didn't need the tiny amusement park to add to her riches. Phipps thereafter donated White City to the Chautauqua association in Bellingham and requested that it be "maintained as a memorial to her father."* She assured Bellingham residents that her father's death and her bequeathing her portion of the Silver Beach property to the Chautauqua would have no effect on the day-

---

* *San Francisco Chronicle*, June 28, 1910.

to-day operation of White City. Later, in August 1910, Phipps and Gwynn agreed that her portion of the ownership of White City would be transferred to the local Chautauqua assembly, as originally intended by Phipps when she received the property through her father's will. However, the donation never occurred. Though Gwynn and Phipps allowed frequent Chautauqua events on the property from 1910 to 1914, the transfer of ownership stalled and never transpired legally. The sale of the land, buildings and fixtures by the White City Amusement Company in 1917 proved that the Chautauqua itself had never received legal ownership. (Main Street in Silver Beach would be renamed Chautaqua—spelled differently than "Chautauqua"—Avenue, and a small portion of it is called that name to this day.)

White City continued its operation. The Labor Day celebration in 1910 included a sack race, apple eating and wood chopping contests, a "largest family" contest, running and high jumping, a peanut race, fifty-yard dashes for both boys and girls, a potato race, ball throwing contests, a shotput contest, a bean guessing contest and a pie eating contest, in addition to the many rides and sights permanently sited at White City. It was all simple, all fun for the locals.

By 1911, the third annual dividend had been paid to White City stockholders—a hefty 6 percent.

John N. Noble acquired the management of the hotel/park complex in April, signing a five-year lease. Gwynn continued as manager of White City except for the food and drink concessions.

On July 4, 1912, a huge fireworks display was set off from a barge in the northern part of Lake Whatcom. The swimming pool and a mechanical ocean wave machine were vigorously advertised. Chautauquas and hot air balloon ascensions continued.

In 1913, small setbacks occurred. The bear cub named Jumbo (one of two cubs) that had been on display in the bear cage was now full-grown, and he began to cause trouble, scaring visitors. Because of his size and the fear that he might escape his cage, both cubs were chained within the cage. A dog that dove into the water from a hot air balloon drowned unexpectedly.

On Labor Day, "moving pictures" became the highlight of the park.

On December 22, after the park closed for the season, the two black bears had to be killed. They were taken to Bellingham, where their skins were displayed for sale at Frye and Company's Market at the corner of Holly Street and Railroad Avenue. Both the fur and the meat were sold at high prices.

By 1915, the ads for White City in the newspapers were becoming noticeably smaller.

The park closed permanently at the end of the 1916 season. The final large picnic at White City was held on July 20. The last ad for the park ran on September 9, though local directories from 1917–18 still listed White City and its owners.

The dismantling of the park occurred in stages. The roller coaster was torn apart, and the lumber was repurposed to other projects in Silver Beach. Charles E. Finzel paid $1,000 for the Ferris wheel, and he shipped it to Ketchikan, Alaska. Later, it was sold again and moved to Prince George, British Columbia.

Over the next seven years, various leases controlled the operation of the hotel, and the name of the hotel reverted to the Silver Beach Hotel.

The hotel and White City were inextricably intertwined, and the hotel continued a slow demise. It's possible that the Spanish flu epidemic of 1918 contributed to its final closure, as quarantines and restrictions on attendance at public places closed many businesses, just as COVID-19 restrictions would do almost a century later. The hotel's financial viability faltered throughout 1918–19.

Ethel B. Henika purchased the land, the hotel and the remnants of the amusement park on June 20, 1917, for $10,000 ("together with all the paraphernalia, equipment, amusement devices, and all other property of every kind and character").* At the time, W.F. Gwynn and Charles S. Gerhart signed for the sale of the Silver Beach Amusement Park as secretary and president of their corporation, respectively. Some reports suggested that Henika was given the property as partial payment for some White City debts; clearly, she purchased it at a bargain price. It included essentially all the waterfront property that is situated on either side of today's Poplar Drive and north to Northshore Drive near Britton Road. Later, as the properties deteriorated, the assessed value of the land and buildings decreased from $3,900 to $3,500 and then to $2,115, in 1923.

By 1922, the hotel was failing to turn a profit. However, coal had been rediscovered underneath the hotel in December 1921, and nearby seams were mined by the Pacific Atomized Fuel Company, which bought or leased the hotel in January 1922 (no records of a sale can be found). The president of this company was Otho H. Williams, and the secretary-treasurer was James L. Gilfilen. The hotel, which was then falling into serious disrepair, became a dormitory for about fifty miners. The first floor had an eating

---

* Whatcom County Auditor's Office, General Index to Recordings and Deed Books. Northwest Regional Branch, Washington State Archives, Bellingham, Washington.

Silver Beach Hotel, viewed from Lake Whatcom wharf. McCaddon and Phillips ice cream store (the second ice cream store; the first, Marshall's Palace, had burned) sits just below and to the right of the hotel. The entrance to White City is at the left. The railroad line is barely visible, but trolley tracks can be seen extending onto the wharf. *Jeffcott Papers, #1588, CPNWS.*

facility and showers; the upper two floors were sleeping rooms. Some say that timbers from the rides at White City were used to support the coal mining tunnels that went underneath Silver Beach. Others say that some White City timbers were simply dumped into the lake. The merry-go-round building became the blacksmith shop; the ice cream store was converted to an equipment shed; the entrance to the mine was located where the roller coaster had been. This coal mining venture also failed. After cessation of mining activity, the hotel was largely abandoned in 1924. Nothing much happened for the next six years, and the hotel was demolished in 1930. Deteriorating further, the hotel was still in Ethel (Mrs. George K.) Henika's possession. It was now useless; its destruction in 1930 made way for homes yet to be built on valuable real estate at the edge of Lake Whatcom.

Henika, then described as a widow, sold the land—the hotel property and twenty-four additional lots in Silver Beach—to Otto S. Kirschner for $100 "and other consideration" on September 28, 1931, the deal being recorded on October 1, 1931.* It's unclear what that "other consideration" might have been. Since this sale was of a huge piece of valuable land, and Henika had spent $10,000 to buy it in 1917, the deal seems unusual. She also included

---

* Tax and Title Records, Northwest Regional Branch, Washington State Archives, Bellingham, Washington.

Silver Beach Hotel from the Northern Pacific Railroad track after the ballroom had been added. White City amusement park rides can be seen on the right. *Whatcom Museum, 2002.0032.000008.*

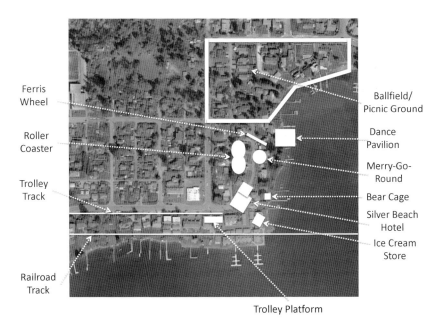

Relationship of current-day structures to the Silver Beach Hotel. *Adapted from Sanborn Maps, CP.NWS, and CityIQ Map, City of Bellingham.*

Entrance to White City (sign reads, "Silver Beach Amusement Park") alongside the Silver Beach Hotel. The McCaddon & Phillips ice cream parlor sits to the right, next to the railroad tracks. *Whatcom Museum, 2001.0012.000003.*

Large crowd at a Puget Sound Traction, Light & Power and Pacific Northwest Traction employee picnic, White City Amusement Park, July 21, 1916. *Biery Papers #1327, CPNWS.*

Today's Northshore Drive where it curves to the north at the site of the Silver Beach Grocery. Then Northshore was called Hastings (east–west; 1904 Sanborn map) or, later, Alabama (1913 Sanborn map). The north–south portion of Northshore was called Main (1904 Sanborn map; now its extension is called Chautaqua). Poplar was then called Argyle. The Bloedel-Donovan (B-D) Lumber Mill can be seen in the background. Academy was initially named Bennett Street on the west side of the lake and Hill Street on the east side. The roller coaster is one street removed east from what is now Northshore. That road is now a north–south alleyway between Northshore and Poplar. *Whatcom Museum, 1996.0010.008830.*

The north end of Lake Whatcom just north of the White City Amusement Park was a ballfield/picnic area, roughly where Britton Road now intersects with Northshore Drive. Grocers' Day picnic, 1910. *Whatcom Museum, 2008.0066.000009.*

White City Dance Pavilion at the edge of Lake Whatcom during Grocers' Day Picnic, 1910. *From Matt Benoit, "Remembering Bellingham's Forgotten 'White City' Amusement Park," WhatcomTalk, November 11, 2019, citing Kent Holsather and Wesley Gannaway,* Bellingham Then and Now *(Bellingham, WA: LoneJack Mountain Press, 2008), 94.*

Panoramic view of Bloedel-Donovan Mills and Silver Beach, circa 1925. White City has been dismantled. The Silver Beach Hotel still exists, but it is difficult to see in this photo. The Northern Pacific Railway crosses Lake Whatcom at the lower left. The new Silver Beach School, built in 1911 on Academy Street, is the brick structure at the center right, while the old school (at this time Squire's Home for the Aged) can be seen just to the left of the new school. *Whatcom Museum, 2002.0077.000042.*

whatever was left of the hotel and the amusement park—"together with all the paraphernalia, equipment, amusement devices, mining equipment and machinery and all other property of every kind and character owned by said Grantor [Henika] and situated upon said real estate; And together with all mineral rights including natural gas and oil."

Other resorts would arise around Lake Whatcom, but none so great as White City.

Geneva

The early town of Geneva was a site of logging, lumber mills, shingle mills and coal mining. Geneva boasted the Geneva Lumber Company, the Bellingham Lumber Company and the Nicholas Jerns Shingle Mill (located slightly west of Geneva town proper). The Geneva wharf was completed on March 8, 1892. The Geneva Mill Company was incorporated on March 16, 1893.

The original landholder sold the land where Geneva would be developed to the Jenkins families in 1886. The Jenkinses were prominent in the early history of the area. Will D. Jenkins and his wife, Elvira A. Jenkins, had three children, David C. Jenkins, Will D. Jenkins Jr. and Lulu Jenkins. George A. Jenkins had his homestead in an area designated as South Geneva; Richard Watkins, also an early settler on Lake Whatcom, had his home in West Geneva. Leslie A. Jenkins homesteaded Reveille Island.

Geneva was dedicated as a town on October 14, 1887, by David Calum Jenkins (son of Will Jenkins); his wife, Elizabeth Jenkins; and Will D. Jenkins and his wife, Elvira A. Jenkins. It was named by David C. Jenkins in 1887 because of its perceived similarity to Geneva, Switzerland. Streets were named after famous explorers: Columbus, Coronado, Stanley, Lewis, Clark, Fremont, etc. Original lots were sold in half-acre to five-acre plots.

In March 1888, the town of Geneva had grown to such a size that fifteen to twenty children were living there, so a school was formed. The first post office opened on July 24, 1888.

At Geneva, the barge was built for the coal-carrying railcars from Blue Canyon. G.B. Peavey was the contractor for this ferry barge, owned and used by the Bellingham Bay and Eastern Railroad, built at Thompson's Mill in Geneva.

Travel to Geneva was complicated before the development of adequate roads. Usually, a traveler would go from Bellingham to Silver Beach by road,

Amended plat of Geneva, 1889. The original plat surveyed by O.B. Iverson had been approved on October 14, 1887. *Whatcom County Tax Parcel Viewer.*

trolley or train, then by boat to Strawberry Point, where a trail led from there to Geneva. The Jenkins family envisioned Geneva as a destination resort with parks and entertainment.

By December 1888, the steamer *Geneva* was making frequent, regular runs along Lake Whatcom, and the wharf at Geneva was completed in March 1892. The Bowery was one of the first entertainment venues in the town, a lumber shed converted to a dance floor in July 1902. Phone service came to Geneva in January 1905, but only five lines were allotted to the entire town.

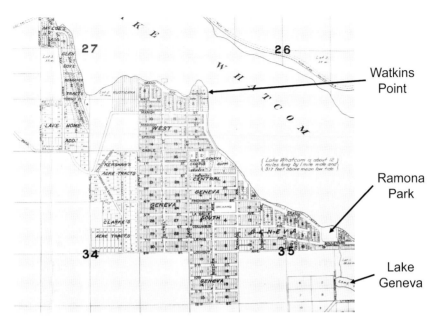

Early plan for Geneva. Ramona Park was situated between Watkins Point and Echo Point (today called Strawberry Point). *E.S. Hincks, Map of the City of Bellingham, Whatcom County, Washington, 1912, Miscellaneous Map Collection, Map #4-3, CPNWS.*

By 1909, the population of Geneva was larger than that of Silver Beach, and by 1911, George Jenkins was advertising round trips on both the *Ramona* and the *Geneva* from Silver Beach/White City to "the head of the lake" (at Park, forty cents), Reveille Island (twenty-five cents) and Ramona Park (fifteen cents). At Ramona Park there was a "fine dance pavilion" and all conveniences for picnicking. Buying a round-trip ticket entitled the ticket holder to use the facilities at these resort places. Jenkins called Lake Whatcom "the most beautiful lake in the world."

Sunnyside/Towanda

Current-day Sunnyside is the area around North Lake Whatcom Park, just north of Smith Creek. Though shown on some maps as a town or village, it never was incorporated.

Woodlawn

Woodlawn was a town envisioned for the area around Agate Bay. Like some other proposed towns around Lake Whatcom, it never really materialized as a distinct entity.

Woodlawn's early commercial life consisted mostly of logging, though a small coal seam also initially attracted interest. Loggers built a small lumber railroad spur extending approximately three miles eastward from Lake Whatcom into the forest to William McCush's logging claim. This railroad antedated the Bellingham Bay and Eastern Railroad around the north and east side of Lake Whatcom by six to eight years. Logs were pulled to the railroad spur by oxen, then loaded on the railroad and subsequently dumped into the lake. Later, the railroad bed was used as a skid road and ultimately became part of current-day Y Road.

Idlewild

Idlewild was another town to be developed north of Agate Bay. It was never developed.

Blue Canyon

Blue Canyon, as a town, was initially entirely dependent on the coal mine. There was no other source of employment or income. Lumbering was nearby, but Blue Canyon was a company town whose existence was coal.

The town had a three-story hotel. There was also a boardinghouse, a school and a saloon. The saloon had disappeared by 1889, as it was frowned upon by the mine directors. It became the J.P. Custer Brothers General Store and Post Office. While hard liquor was prohibited by the mine rules (Blue Canyon was, after all, a "company town"), the Custer brothers had a keg of beer imported from Silver Beach to their establishment every Saturday for the miners. Custer's store would eventually be moved to Park in 1906. The Blue Canyon school at its peak had about forty pupils, in the town of about one thousand residents. The schoolhouse itself was also used for church gatherings and town meetings. It was physically moved to Park after the mine closed and Blue Canyon's population dwindled.

Blue Canyon began to wane as the coal mining disappeared. By 1918, the Bellingham Coal Mine had begun operation near Bellingham Bay, and it soon became clear that the coal there was more abundant, higher quality and closer to distribution points. Blue Canyon saw its residents move away, and the railroad service even decreased. Some residents moved slightly farther southeast to Park, but Park never flourished, in part because it was remote from any attractions or employment opportunities, except for lumbering, which was itself moving farther and farther away from Lake Whatcom. As the mining at Blue Canyon slowed to insufficient levels to sustain the families there, Bloedel, Donovan and Larson convinced many of the residents to convert to logging as a profession.

Park

Park was never incorporated like Silver Beach and Geneva. It was originally named Anderson's Landing, after Michael Anderson. One of the original settlers, Fred Zobrist, owned and ran the general store at Park.

Park was always overshadowed by nearby Blue Canyon. Lumber mills between Park and Wickersham were the E.K. Wood Lumber Mill and the Knight Timber Company. Shingle mills also factored into the local economy.

The railroad eventually came to Blue Canyon, and in 1901, it connected Blue Canyon to Wickersham and Acme through Park. As the railroad expanded, some houses that had been constructed on the railroad right-of-way had to be moved or demolished. Apparently, the homeowners had not believed that the railroad would actually extend as far as planned.

As the city of Blue Canyon's viability plummeted with the closure of the coal mine, some of its residents slowly migrated back to nearby Park. Never a commercial center, Park had only what would today be called a convenience store. A small auto/motorcycle repair business opened, but like the rest of the town, it too was destined for smallness. The business briefly became the center of a county council debate about zoning laws, and the zoning was finally changed to allow the store, but because the region was in the Lake Whatcom watershed, no car or motorcycle repair was allowed for fear of gasoline and oil washing into the lake. Even the Park Post Office moved to Silver Beach in 1911.

South Bay

South Bay was a site for logging, and it briefly boasted a coal mining claim, though not enough coal was present for commercial use. South Bay never developed into a town itself.

South Bay School was located on land formerly owned by John L. Miller.*

Wickersham

Though technically Wickersham is outside the boundaries usually associated with Lake Whatcom, it was connected to the economy of the lake. Named after Noah and Will Wickersham—the original settlers on the land, who came in about 1885 from Kansas—it started as two forty-acre plots of land, one donated by each of the Wickershams to develop a town after the railroad came to the area. Initially, the stage connected the steamships on Lake Whatcom from Blue Canyon to Wickersham through Park.

Wickersham was on the rail line from Seattle to Sumas and then Canada, and the railroad around Lake Whatcom purposely connected to that system so it would have access to the north and the south.

Lumber and shingle production had been prominent at the inception of Wickersham, but now the region has become farmland. It currently houses an antique railroad that runs a short distance on the old Northern Pacific route.

Sudden Valley

One of the largest land-use developments around Lake Whatcom was the housing consortium called Sudden Valley. The land was owned by Banning Austin, who sold it to Glen and Betty Corning in 1949. In 1968, the Cornings sold 1,200 acres of their property to Ken Sanwick. Sanwick originally wanted to keep much of the land in its native state while building a few homes in the midst of the natural beauty.

Development took over as the first plat for a large group of homes was approved in 1969. The Sudden Valley Community Club was incorporated in August 1973. After sequential sales to various owners, SunMark Inc. assumed control in 1973, followed by Continental Mortgage Investors in

---

* S ½ NE ¼, Section 29, Township 37 N, Range 4 E.

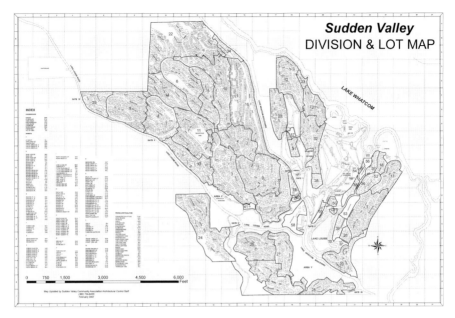

Sudden Valley plat map, February 2007. *Whatcom County Tax Parcel Viewer.*

1976. Following a series of financial disasters, the development was taken over by the Sudden Valley Community Association. This association was responsible for the purchase and development of many amenities on the properties, such as a golf course, a swimming pool, parks, playgrounds, greenbelts, a marina, an aquatic airstrip, a library, hiking trails and a country club.

Sudden Valley has become one of the largest cooperative homeowners' associations in the state of Washington and, indeed, in the United States. Today, over eight thousand persons live in this area.

Chapter 12

SCHOOLS AROUND LAKE WHATCOM

GENEVA

The first school in Geneva was built in 1890 and located on the east side of Austin Street, south of Cable Street. A second structure followed it in 1891. Times were hard in the 1890s, and the Geneva school occasionally had to close for lack of funds. The current building on Geneva Street was constructed in 1982, with an addition in 1992. One of the original school buildings became the Geneva Community Center.

SILVER BEACH

As Silver Beach developed and grew, a school was established at the southeast corner of Pullman and Academy. The first school (of which no photos exist) was opened on October 20, 1890, with twelve pupils. A new schoolhouse—the first building dedicated for use as such—was opened on January 28, 1892, at the same location, but it was destroyed by a forest fire in 1894. A new building (the third school, though perhaps only the second dedicated school building) was quickly constructed by 1895. This third schoolhouse was abandoned sixteen years later, and a new one—the first brick school building in the town of Silver Beach—was dedicated on January 5, 1912. (The abandoned wooden schoolhouse was converted to Squire's Home for the

Above: An 1891 photo of the First Geneva School, built in 1890. *Whatcom Museum, 2008.0091.000006.*

Left: Silver Beach School, circa 1892–94, front view. This building was the second structure used for the school, though it was the first dedicated for use solely as a schoolhouse. No photos exist of the first building used as a schoolhouse. *Biery Papers, #2291, CPNWS.*

Silver Beach School, a brick structure located at 4101 Academy, constructed in 1911 and dedicated on January 6, 1912. *Whatcom Museum, 2007.0021.000001.*

Silver Beach School (Wood Frame – Constructed 1895)

Silver Beach School (Brick – Constructed 1911)

Above: Aerial photo of two Silver Beach Schools, circa 1925, showing a brick structure at the corner of Academy and Pullman and a wooden structure lower on Pullman, which by this time was Squire's Home for the Aged. *Whatcom Museum, 2002.0077.000042.*

Opposite: South Bay School; photo taken in 1897. *Whatcom Museum, 1985.0023.000001.*

Aged, opening on December 17, 1914, and later repurposed as a children's home. It was eventually abandoned and later burned on October 22, 1928.) The brick structure—the fourth Silver Beach School—was originally designed as a wood frame building with a footprint of sixty-nine by ninety feet. Its three stories included a ground-level basement, and the upper two floors had four classrooms, each twenty-five by thirty-two feet. Construction began in the summer of 1911, at which time the design was changed to brick, with an estimated total cost of $14,900. The school's design was said to be the most modern and scientific available. This building burned on July 21, 1954, due to combustion of fumes from a varnish remover, but the fire was contained to the top floor. Already under construction just to the east of the brick building was a new school annex, and it was quickly pressed into service, with a dedication on October 6, 1954. The 1911 brick structure was demolished in 1994 to make way for a newer building.

Today's school was built in three stages: 1954, 1978 and 1993–94.

South Bay

The South Bay school system was organized on January 3, 1891. The first teacher in this district was Clara Belle Foster; the first teacher in this building, a one-room schoolhouse, was Charles E. Kagay.

Blue Canyon

The first teacher came to Blue Canyon from New Whatcom by boat and, later, by rail. The school term was four to six months, with the teacher going to another district for the other portion of the year. As many as ninety students were eligible for the school at the height of Blue Canyon's population, although the average class size was only twenty to thirty students.

The schoolhouse was used as the local church on Sundays.

Chapter 13

RESORTS AND GATHERING PLACES

BLOEDEL-DONOVAN PARK (2214 ELECTRIC AVENUE)

Bloedel-Donovan Park originated with a donation from the Bloedel family. This twelve-and-a-half-acre site was donated in September 1946 as a gift from Julius and Mina Bloedel, along with $150,000 to develop the property. The family specified that the land was to be used solely for the recreational purposes of the people of Bellingham and that the park would forever be called Bloedel-Donovan Park. The park was dedicated on August 11, 1948, the fiftieth anniversary of the founding of the Lake Whatcom Logging Company.

After the establishment of the park, the Bloedels continued to contribute to its development. The park eventually expanded to 17.76 acres. By 1950 a parking lot was added, and a boat launch soon followed. In March 1960, the Bloedel Foundation (Julius Bloedel had died on September 21, 1957) gave $26,443 to enlarge the park and improve the swimming area; in January 1962, the Bloedel Foundation gave $5,201 to construct a swimming float and diving board. The caretaker's home was converted to a preschool in 1980. The swimming area was improved in 2021. The boat launch was improved in 1983 with funds from the Washington State Recreation Program.

For many years, the park had boasted a 1918 No. 9 H.K. Porter steam railroad engine, designated "Old Number 7"—a switcher engine. The Permanente Cement Company had originally purchased it from the U. S. Navy, and Permanente gave it to the City of Bellingham in 1960 as part of historic preservation efforts. It was moved to the Northwest Railway Museum in Snoqualmie in 2017.

Bloedel-Donovan Park. *Adapted from CityIQ Map, City of Bellingham.*

The park now has open fields, a boat dock, a boat launch for powerboats, a hand-carry launch for canoes and kayaks, a conference and meeting center with space for 200 people, a 700-square-foot pavilion with seating for 50, a kitchen, a 4,368-square-foot gymnasium, children's playgrounds, volleyball courts, access to fishing, a preschool building, a swimming area with a large H-shaped dock located in the water just east of the Electric Avenue bridge, a boat rental center and the Whatcom Rowing Association Boathouse, a basketball court, an off-leash dog area, a ball field, picnic sites and tables, barbecue grills, parking, restroom facilities, trails and heritage trees. It sits next to Whatcom Falls Park, another hiking and nature facility, and parking is available.

SCUDDER POND
(ELECTRIC AVENUE AND ALABAMA STREET)

Scudder Pond is a relatively new entity, likely formed by the activity of beavers that blocked a culvert that drained into Lake Whatcom. The small pond appeared in aerial photos between 1963 and 1975. It gradually enlarged and became the size it is today. The land for this 2.8-acre nature preserve was donated in 1987 by Vida Disbrow Armitage to the North Cascades Audubon Society in honor of her father, Oliver Clarence Scudder

(1879–1945), a Bellingham businessman and real estate dealer. The deed to the nature preserve was transferred to the City of Bellingham in 2014.

Scudder Pond has trails and is a nature/wildlife preserve, with interpretive signs that explain the area's wildlife, birds and plant life. This small park is home to many bird species, including red-winged blackbirds, ducks, Virginia rails, mallards, buffleheads, wood ducks and great blue herons. Its trails connect to Whatcom Falls Park (with its Railroad Trails) and Bloedel-Donovan Park.

Whatcom Falls Park (1401 Electric Avenue)

In 1911, a group of investors recognized that a plot of land was soon to become available for sale and that it would make an ideal city park. However, the city was moving slowly, and it looked like the opportunity to acquire the property for the city might be missed. So this group of men, including Bloedel, Donovan and twelve others, purchased the property to protect it from other investors. Soon thereafter, they resold it to the City of Bellingham. It is located opposite Bloedel-Donovan Park on Electric Avenue.

Whatcom Falls Park, circa 1892. *Whatcom Museum, 1973.0035.000016.*

Whatcom Falls Park is 251 acres of wooded trails following Whatcom Creek and the Railroad Trails. It has a bridge built with Chuckanut sandstone in 1939 by the Works Progress Administration. Derby Pond is a stocked fishing site available to children. The park has a ball field with a backstop, a basketball court, a bicycle pump track, covered and uncovered picnic areas with benches, restrooms, two playfields, tennis courts, a 1,344-square-foot shelter that seats up to seventy-two, an 800-square-foot shelter that seats twenty-four, a fish hatchery and the Bellingham water purification plant. Extensive pathways (some of which are old railroad rights-of-way) are used by walkers, joggers, strollers and bicyclists. The old Milwaukee Railroad wooden trestle, built in 1916, was located within the park. Because it was deteriorating, it was demolished in September 2023.

Limited parking is available.

Euclid Park
(Between Euclid Avenue and Lakeway Drive)

Euclid Park sits just to the west of Geneva Elementary School. It is heavily treed and has limited water access, with a small and primitive trail system. Only two to four parking spots are available, depending on vehicle size.

Lookout Mountain Park and Forest Preserve

Lookout Mountain Forest Preserve is situated at the far southwestern end of the lake. It has 338 acres, and it is adjacent to 4,251 acres of reconveyed Department of Natural Resources land. Its parking lot, accessible from Lake Louise Road at Polo Park Drive, accommodates twenty-nine cars, and it has public restrooms. While the park never completely touches the edge of Lake Whatcom, it skirts the edge along South Lake Whatcom Boulevard.

Lake Whatcom Park

Lake Whatcom Park is situated at the far southeastern end of the lake where Northshore Road terminates. It has 207 acres, including the Chanterelle Trail, and it is adjacent to 4,593 acres of reconveyed Department of Natural Resources land. Two parking lots lead to the Hertz Trail, which traces the path of the Blue Canyon railroad line initially built by the Bellingham Bay and Eastern Railway (later bought by the Northern Pacific Railway). Trails are used by walkers, hikers, bicyclists and joggers. Small beaches along the route are ideal for small picnics, swimming or launching kayaks or canoes. The trail ends before the abandoned site of the Blue Canyon Coal Mine. The two parking lots accommodate forty-five cars, and a restroom is located at the northeastern parking facility. Backcountry camping sites are also available.

Stimpson Family Nature Reserve

The Stimpson Family Nature Reserve is located to the north of Lookout Mountain Park. It has four miles of hiking trails that meander through some old-growth forest of four-hundred-year-old Douglas fir. The access point is a trailhead on Lake Louise Road, with another local access in Sudden Valley. It includes Beaver Pond and Geneva Pond, and a parking lot can be accessed off Lake Louise Road. Deer, cougar and beavers can be seen here.

Galbraith Mountain

Galbraith Mountain, located to the northwest of Lookout Mountain Park, technically does not border Lake Whatcom, but it is partially within the Lake Whatcom watershed. This land is a popular mountain biking destination, and it is well-known throughout the United States among mountain biking enthusiasts. A portion of it covers the site of the old Geneva Coal Mine, though remnants of that mine have disappeared. Trails cover 2,500 acres of private timberland, yielding over fifty miles of mountain biking paths.

Big Rock Garden (2900 Sylvan Street)

This park is hidden in a local neighborhood, boasting two and a half acres with an adjacent nine-and-a-half-acre open space. The sculpture garden and artistic displays are created by local and international artists, punctuated by gorgeous plants, shrubs and trees. The park has a gazebo, trails, a drinking fountain, parking and restrooms.

Smaller Parks/Lake Access

Smaller public access points exist around the perimeter of the lake: Silver Beach Open Space (between Maynard Place and Silvern Lane), Connecticut Street Access (end of Connecticut Street), North Street Access (end of North Street) and Donald Avenue Access (end of Donald Avenue).

Each of these access points allows entry to Lake Whatcom, though parking is restricted or nonexistent. Swimming, fishing and sunbathing access is available. These sites are frequently used for launching kayaks, canoes and other small water toys.

Other small beaches are private and/or part of homeowners' associations, not accessible to the general public: Maynard Place Beach (end of Maynard Place) and Silver Shores Beach (end of Silvern Lane).

Wildwood Resort

Wildwood Resort (also called Wildwood Park) was begun as another private recreational area after its early life as a lumber mill. It was never intended to be like the Silver Beach/White City amusement park; it was envisioned as a site for boating, fishing, camping and small retreat houses and cabins. Located on South Bay, its distance from other loci of activity worked against its growth. It is occupied now almost exclusively in the summer, and it has a swimming pool, a clubhouse, tennis court, a marina with about fifty boat slips, a boat launch, recreational vehicle and camping sites and a swimming area.

The Firs

The Firs began in July 1921 when Otis Grant Whipple and his wife, Julia, had a five-day retreat at their cabin overlooking Lake Whatcom in what today is Geneva. The building where the retreat was held was a small twenty-by-twenty-foot cottage built in 1903. After this original gathering and some encouragement from friends, they decided to make the meeting an annual event. Eventually, the Whipples made the property a retreat center, initially calling it the Lake Whatcom Bible and Missionary Conference and incorporating as a nonprofit entity on June 7, 1927. Later, it would be called the Firs Bible and Missionary Conference. Geneva Community Church began here in 1952; in 2000, the church moved to the corner of McLeod and Britton Roads as Northlake Community Church.

The directors realized that for young people to have a successful camping experience, the retreat needed a larger property with more water access, as well as a more rustic location. In 1954, a group of junior-high-school-age campers gathered on the property of Glen Corning, located near Reveille Island (technically at 1740 Lake Whatcom Boulevard). This 80.98-acre site would become what is now Camp Firwood (it was initially dubbed White Sands). The Firs purchased this land the next year (1955) for $35,000, and the 4,500 feet of shoreline became the center for youth retreats and camps. Sandwiched between Lake Louise and Reveille Island, the retreat center also included Reveille Island itself. At this time, there were no roads leading to the site, and everything had to be brought to the location by boat.

The Fircreek Day Camp began in 1960 at the original Retreat Center. The Firs Chalet at Mount Baker was part of the organization's wide-ranging ministry, opening in 1958. Yet another branch of this outreach was the After School Adventure program that began in 2001.

Today, the Firs continues to operate from the Geneva area, with the Firs Retreat Center (8.5 acres with its own beach, accommodating groups of 25–220 year-round), Camp Firwood (nine weeks of camping for grades 3–12), the Firs Chalet at Mt. Baker (open year-round for high school juniors up to adults), Fircreek Day Camp (during the summer for grades 1–6) and the After School Adventure (during school times for grades K–5).

Agate Bay Resort

Many other private recreational sites appeared around the lake, though none so elaborate as White City. The Agate Bay Resort offered cabins, boating and swimming as the chief entertainments. It flourished briefly but eventually closed.

Chapter 14

OTHER RECREATION

FISHING

Fishing was one activity that initially drew men to the area. The *Northern Light* reported on the beauties of Lake Whatcom in 1858:

> *It is some five or six miles south-east of Whatcom, although very difficult of approach, owing to the many obstacles encountered on the trail.*

The water was

> *clear as crystal, sweet to the taste, cold, and, in some places, of fathomless depth. Ten miles from its south-western outlet, an island, seven or eight hundred feet high, a quarter of a mile wide, by about a mile in length, is reached; on the shores of which, perhaps, the finest trout fishing in the world is found. These fish bite with great voracity, and are easily taken with good bait, by means of hook and line. Those which our party captured, would weigh from half a pound to three and four pounds. Several strong lines were broken, however, in the attempt to bring others to shore, which leads to the conclusion that there must be much larger fish in the lake—weighing, probably, from eight to ten pounds.*
>
> *If a good wagon road were cut through to this Lake, and a comfortable hotel erected on, or in the near vicinity of the island, provided with suitable pleasure boats, no spot on the Pacific coast could be more desirable as a place of summer resort. The Lake lies walled in between mountains,*

*abounding with deer (several of which were seen drinking at the beach),
and is certainly one of the most picturesque spots which ever gave brilliancy
or romance to a landscape.*

Lake Whatcom was abundantly supplied with trout, and Clarence H. Chandler came to Lake Whatcom in 1906 to fish with his friend William Gwynn. His experience prompted him to invest $100,000 in the development of Silver Beach and White City.

While the fishing and canning industries were prominent on Bellingham Bay and provided a major source of income, no such activities could be found on Lake Whatcom. Sport fishing was abundantly available, but it did not compete with coal, timber or entertainment for commercial activity.

To maintain this recreational attraction, the lake has been repeatedly stocked with fish. As early as 1907, the federal government stocked the lake with trout. A trout hatchery was well established at Lake Whatcom by 1911.

Today, Lake Whatcom has thirteen species of fish, six of which are native to the lake: Kokanee salmon, cutthroat trout, longnose sucker, peamouth chub, sculpin and threespine stickleback. Bluegill, rainbow trout and smallmouth bass have been purposely introduced by the Fish and Game Department. Today, the most common species to be caught in the lake are brown bullhead, cutthroat trout, Kokanee salmon, largemouth bass, peamouth chub, pumpkinseed sunfish, smallmouth bass and yellow perch.

Some invasive species of plants, animals and pathogens, especially various types of mussels (zebra and quagga mussels), have been inadvertently added to the lake, and boats must be inspected annually to ensure that further lake contamination is avoided.

HUNTING

In the mid- and late 1800s, hunting was a common subsistence activity. Native Americans and early settlers found abundant deer and less common elk, bear (both black and grizzly, though the grizzly had essentially disappeared by 1900), cougar, bobcat, raccoon, rabbits and some beaver and nutria.

Migratory waterfowl included duck, coot, snipe, pigeon and goose. Others less transient were dove, grouse, turkey, pheasant, quail and partridge, and even crow and owl were hunted.

Today, because of the encroachment of towns and homes, hunting is mostly prohibited.

Chapter 15

LAKE WHATCOM

Bellingham's Water Source

The founders of Fairhaven/Bellingham/Sehome/Whatcom in the 1880s realized the value of Lake Whatcom as a source of water. The outflow of Lake Whatcom then was estimated to be about five million to eight million gallons of water per day during the dry season, and one hundred million gallons per day during the wet season. It was the ideal source of water for their burgeoning communities, but it was about three miles away as the creek flowed. Residents of these towns had been using water from the many streams in the area, and wells were common. One had only to dig a short distance down to strike water that could suffice for a large homestead. However, the communities were growing, and all needed a more reliable water source. Because Lake Whatcom was outside the city limits of all four towns, officials were unsure if they had jurisdiction to construct water control and distribution systems there.

Whatcom Creek also fed the lumber mill where the creek dumped into Bellingham Bay, the site of Russell V. Peabody's 1853 donation claim along the shore. Peabody had constructed this sawmill and dam in 1853–54, using the water from Whatcom Creek to power the saws, which could process seventy-five thousand feet of lumber per day. The mill required about 2.5 million gallons per hour for efficient operation. Because the flow of water in Whatcom Creek varied greatly with the season, the quantity was insufficient to power the mill during dry times. The mill burned in 1873, and in 1882–83, the lumber mill was rebuilt about fifty yards from the old sawmill site. The Fairhaven Land Company (FLC) eventually took ownership of this property in about 1889 and built a small dam at its own expense at the outlet of Lake Whatcom, the beginning of the control of the effluent from the lake.

The Bellingham Bay Water Company (BBWC) was formed to provide clean water to the communities around Bellingham Bay. Its first meeting was held on June 18, 1883, with Edward Eldridge as chairman and Herman H. Hofercamp as secretary. Hugh Eldridge completed the group of three trustees. Soon, they agreed to finance the company by selling ten thousand shares of stock at ten dollars each. Pierre B. Cornwall became the president of the company; hence, it was often called the Cornwall System. One of the company's first purchases was a $200 expenditure to obtain the rights to lay water pipes along the properties of Mr. and Mrs. Edward Eldridge and Mr. Erastus Bartlett. It was May 1884 before the company petitioned the City of Whatcom to allow the placement of pipes along the streets and alleyways of the town. The Whatcom City Council granted a fifty-year nonexclusive franchise to the company, but the grant was vetoed. In June 1885, the men reapplied, and in July, they were given a forty-five-year nonexclusive approval. Nelson Bennett's forces obtained an injunction to prevent the BBWC from developing this project because of the potential adverse effects on his downstream interests in the Whatcom Creek area. By September, the injunction had been lifted, but the Whatcom City Council still needed to give final approval for construction. A rudimentary system was begun, and by December 1885, some water was already being delivered to Whatcom by makeshift conduits. These early temporary water systems connected Lake Whatcom with the communities along Bellingham Bay. The first intake pipe to deliver water to the towns was located within Lake Whatcom, with early portions of the steel pipe following the banks of Whatcom Creek for about half a mile. That pipe was destroyed by high water only a few months later, when the origin was moved into the creek itself, about a quarter of a mile downstream from the outlet of Lake Whatcom but still above Whatcom Falls. A new pipe would later be installed about a quarter of a mile above the outlet of the lake and on its east side, and the first "permanent" pipe would be located in approximately the same location above the outlet of Lake Whatcom at the Bloedel-Donovan Mills. All pipes were described as running parallel to Whatcom Creek, though their precise course is unknown today.

It was not until January 30, 1889, that the BBWC approved hiring a superintendent for construction and adding laborers to begin the formal work on the project as designed. Whatcom was still hesitant to approve waterworks construction, but Sehome passed Ordinance No. 25 on

March 7, 1889, authorizing the delivery of water throughout the city, beginning at Elk and Maple Streets. It required guaranteed water pressure of at least 150 pounds per square inch, and the agreement included the placement of fire hydrants at every street corner. This pressure was expected to generate a vertical column of water at least seventy-five feet high, useful for fighting fires.

Laying of new pipes for a revision of the makeshift system began later in 1889, after delineation of the right-of-way for burying these conduits. The easement for such use near Lake Whatcom was secured by a contract executed on April 3, 1889, between the BBWC and Henry McCue, owner of government lot no. 5 on the edge of Lake Whatcom (part of which would ultimately be occupied by the Bloedel-Donovan Lumber Mill). The agreement specified a fifty-foot easement where the company could "dig ditches, lay pipes, build flumes, bore tunnels, and construct conduits" for the water system. In 1889–90, the company dug some shafts vertically to determine the quality of the soil through which the tunnel would need to be dug and to see if large rocks might interfere with the construction of the tunnels necessary to hold the pipes.

Not to be outdone by Sehome, the Whatcom City Council finally approved Ordinance No. 93 on July 9, 1889, which likewise contracted with the BBWC to supply the city of Whatcom with fresh water. It specified that the water system would enter the city at the corner of Thirteenth and E Streets, and a fire hydrant was also to be placed at each intersection. Fire control and prevention were crucial to cities of this era. Bellingham and other parts of Whatcom County were added to this system later in 1889. The Fairhaven water supply was to come from Lake Padden, via a separate company established in October 1889 (the Fairhaven Water Company). The projected completion date for the Lake Padden system was May 15, 1890.

The BBWC began the construction of a road to the Lake Whatcom site in April 1889. It terminated at lot no. 5 near the outlet of Lake Whatcom, that land owned by Henry McCue. The BBWC worked toward laying the pipe to the corner of Maple and Railroad Streets (slightly removed from its original target) in New Whatcom. The first water sold within the city by the BBWC was in March 1890, even before the five-hundred-foot tunnel was dug from Lake Whatcom to a site along Whatcom Creek in 1894.

On August 8, 1889, the FLC served the BBWC with a notice to cease activity around Lake Whatcom. It claimed that construction of the water system would adversely affect its ability to run its sawmill at the end of Whatcom Creek. It needed about twenty-five million gallons of water per day to run

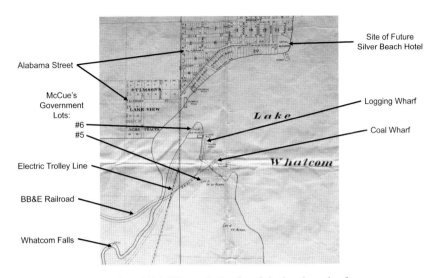

North Lake Whatcom, circa 1904. The coal wharf and the logging wharf were separate. Note that Alabama Street is discontinuous. Dakin Street and Hastings Street connect the two segments of Alabama Street. The BB&E Railroad did not yet cross the northern end of Lake Whatcom. The CMStP&P railway had not yet been built. *Bellingham Bay Improvement Company Records, Map #9-10, CPNWS.*

the mill (2.5 million gallons per hour for ten hours). The FLC itself had been blasting along the course of the creek, and it was constructing another dam to modulate the flow of water into its sawmill, to increase flow during dry months and decrease it during wet months. Judge Cornelius H. Hanford issued a restraining order to prevent the BBWC from entering the creek with its project. The BBWC obtained a counter-injunction against the FLC to prevent the FLC from entering land leased by the BBWC for its project. The BBWC argued that its use of water would not substantially affect the water level of either the lake or the creek and, furthermore, that the FLC owners were actually shareholders in the BBWC and had encouraged the BBWC to pursue its plan to develop the water supply for the cities downstream from Lake Whatcom. The original FLC lawsuit began in August 1889 in the District Court of Whatcom County, Washington Territory. By June 1890, the lawsuit was still far from being settled.

In June 1891, the city of Whatcom expressed interest in buying the BBWC for its own operation. On December 22, 1892, Whatcom passed a bond issue to fund the purchase of the water system from the BBWC by a vote of 678 to 209. New Whatcom finally bought the BBWC for $144,699.33 on September 15, 1893. Thereafter, the intake pipes were soon moved into the lake proper, the new pipes mostly twenty-four inches in diameter at a depth of about twenty feet. This intake drew water from the lake just at the eastern edge of the Bloedel-Donovan mills, then called Larson's Mill. It delivered water through pipes along Lake Street (now called Lakeway), through the Bay View Cemetery, to James Street and then to Holly and State Streets. (Only later would the water company construct another delivery system along Alabama Street, Cornwall Street, Nicklin Street and finally to North Street.)

The FLC lawsuit worked its way through the courts for years. In 1899, the Superior Court ruled in favor of the FLC, saying that the BBWC had to cease the use of Lake Whatcom water because it had infringed on the "riparian rights" of the downstream users of Whatcom Creek. Countersuits argued that the cities would suffer immeasurably from the loss of their water supply, necessary for the health and safety of their citizens. Clearly, they depended on the water from Lake Whatcom for their existence and survival. Equally clearly, withdrawal of water from the lake and creek caused harm to the owners of the sawmill. In April 1901, the Supreme Court of Washington reversed and modified the ruling. The final judgment declared that the City of New Whatcom (the subsequent owner of the water system and the defendant against claims filed by the FLC suing the BBWC) was allowed to continue its withdrawal of water from Lake Whatcom (on the principle of the power of eminent domain), but the city had to compensate the FLC for any damages incurred from the reduction in waterpower to its mill caused by the removal of large quantities of water from the lake. It faulted the BBWC (and its successor, the City of New Whatcom, which had also assumed its legal liabilities) for initially neglecting to use the power of eminent domain to condemn the property, for not securing the rights to the water and for refusing to compensate the FLC owners for their damages.

By the spring and summer of 1891, however, another dispute had arisen regarding the Lake Whatcom end of the pipeline. The landowner Henry McCue, who had agreed to relinquish a strip of his property for the project, had discovered that the water company had moved the course of the proposed pipeline without his approval after it had already disturbed his land along the course of the original proposed route, destroying trees, digging shafts, creating a road and otherwise transforming his land. The change in course doubled the impact on his property. Furthermore, the company, wanting to avoid any delay in sending water to the towns, had installed a temporary pipe along the course of Whatcom Creek ("along the margin of Lake Whatcom"—which was likely on or near lot no. 6, not lot no. 5). This temporary pipe had been installed within Whatcom Creek, starting about a quarter of a mile below the outlet of Lake Whatcom and about six feet below the level of the origin of Whatcom Creek. The pipe itself ran generally parallel to Whatcom Creek but was at times above the land/creek surface.

McCue argued that the installation of the temporary pipe voided the prior agreement because the company had used land outside the original easement. In addition, the company, in August 1891, was now claiming a different fifty-foot strip of land through McCue's property, destroying yet more of his land. McCue also feared that the construction would leave open trenches into which his cattle and other animals might fall. The company argued that the first pipe was temporary and that it never intended to abandon the easement for the permanent pipeline. It also contended that the temporary pipe did not actually pass through any portion of lot no. 5, so it was irrelevant to discussions about the permanent route. Since the temporary line was below the high-water level of the surface of Lake Whatcom and below the bed of Whatcom Creek, technically, the land on which it had been laid was the property of the state. The issue went to court on November 21, 1891, and McCue's lawsuit was dismissed. Further appeals emerged, and ultimately, the case went to the Supreme Court of the state, which ruled on November 3, 1892, that the original easement route through lot no. 5 had to be employed for the water project, that the water company had not abandoned its agreement with McCue since no time limit for the easement had been specified in the contract and that the temporary line was not actually located in lot no. 5. Further appeals continued until 1901. By 1893, however, the inlet to the temporary water pipeline system was already within Lake Whatcom itself, just east of McCue's lot no. 5.

The "permanent" piping system ultimately began with about 1,300 feet of a thirty-inch main in Lake Whatcom, followed by seven thousand to eight thousand feet of a twenty-four-inch pipe, and then the final eleven-inch conduit to Whatcom and Sehome. The eleven-inch pipe could deliver about 1.5–2 million gallons per day, while the larger thirty-inch pipe at the origin of the system could have delivered about 14 million gallons per day if it had remained at the larger bore for its entire length. The engineers estimated that the withdrawal of this amount of water from the lake would cause it to drop only 1.5 inches in depth during the three months of the dry summer season. Further, they surmised that even this degree of variation in the level of the lake could be mitigated by a dam at the lake's outlet. In practice, the initial use of this system delivered about 1.5 million gallons of water per day.

Intake for the water system, circa 1894. Wooden pipe is being placed in Basin No. 1, near today's Bloedel-Donovan Park. *Whatcom Museum, 1996.0010.003554.*

The Lake Whatcom intake pipe for a time was perilously close to the edge of the lumber mill. As the activity at the Larson Lumber Mill and its successor, the Bloedel-Donovan Lumber Mill, increased, waste, wood particles, sawdust, silt and moss from the mill operations would clog the outflow of the lake into Whatcom Creek, as well as foul the pipes supplying Bellingham. Furthermore, local sewage from the area also inadvertently entered the pipe. In 1903, the pipe broke, and a repair to replace the wooden pipe with a steel structure was scheduled to be completed by July 1, 1904. But early in 1904, the system suffered a catastrophic failure near its origin off the shore at Larson's Mill. Nearly one hundred feet of the thirty-inch wooden pipe collapsed, rendering the newly formed city of Bellingham without a water supply. Immediately on notification of the problem, all industries using this water source were told to cease drawing water from the city's lines. City officials feared that firefighting might suffer if water was needed for an emergency during the outage. The pipe was repaired before any emergency occurred.

One of the major advantages of Lake Whatcom as a water source was the fact that the lake level was over three hundred feet above the level of the

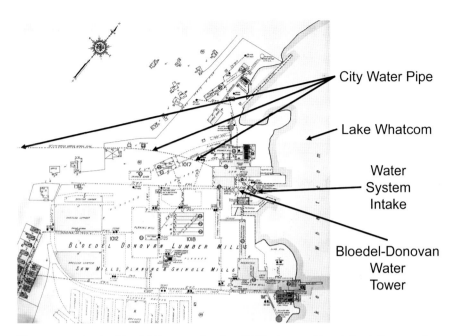

City Water Pipe

Lake Whatcom

Water
System
Intake

Bloedel-Donovan
Water
Tower

Water system intake. Bloedel-Donovan Lumber Mill is shown with a stylized diagram of
the water pipe to Bellingham City. The origin of the pipe in this map is sited at the location
of the intake well, at the shore of the Bloedel-Donovan Lumber Mill; however, the intake
had already been moved into the center of Basin No. 1 of Lake Whatcom, about 1,400 feet
from the shore. *Adapted from Sanborn Map, 1913, CPNWS.*

towns, so gravity supplied sufficient force to deliver the water westward. The
pressure (90–120 pounds per square inch) was even sufficient to allow the
fire department to use it without pumps. Nearby Silver Beach received its
water directly from pumps located at the Bloedel-Donovan Mills.

The 1913 Sanborn map verbally described the water intake port of
the system at Lake Whatcom as a thirty-inch wooden stave pipe (made of
Douglas fir). However, the map itself listed a "40-inch city water works
intake pipe" that appeared to end at the bank of Lake Whatcom in the
Bloedel-Donovan Mill complex, though the actual intake was farther into
the lake. Portions of the city were also served by a 270,000-gallon cemented
stone reservoir. About 40 percent of the pipes in the city at that time were
wooden, the oldest having been installed in 1893.

By 1926, two "intake cribs" were listed as being at 700 and 1,400 feet
from the shore.* The first intake crib had been 700 feet offshore, but it
had been revised by adding intake crib no. 2 to place the inlet farther and

* Thomson, *Report.*

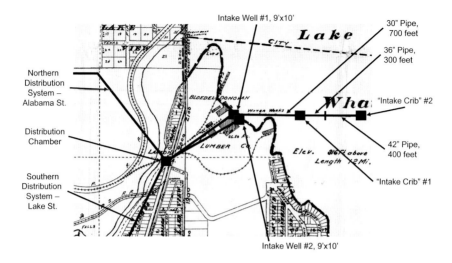

Water system in 1926. Two distribution systems delivered the water to Bellingham. *Adapted from C.M. Adams, Bellingham City Map, 1922, Whatcom Museum, 1995.0022.000001.*

lower into the lake. Crib no. 2 was 85 feet below the lake's surface, but the actual intake was shallower. From intake crib no. 2 coursed a 42-inch pipe for 400 feet, then a 36-inch pipe for 300 feet, followed by the original 700 feet of 30-inch pipe. It entered what was called an intake well (concrete, 9 feet by 10 feet). The new system (1914) had been designed to use a new intake well (no. 2, also concrete) just about 15 feet south of the first one (no. 1). The design had planned for a new pipe to come from the lake, but the revision of the system had continued to use the original intake well and pipe from the lake, requiring the first intake well to dump into the second. From the second intake well, a 30-inch concrete-lined pipe ran 1,427 feet to the "distribution chamber," located "under the Northern Pacific Railway spur."[*] Precisely where it was located under the spur is unclear, but it was likely at the crossing of the spur over Whatcom Creek. This pipe was oval, 4 feet, 7 inches high by 3 feet wide. The entire series of pipes had the capacity to deliver about 45 million gallons of water per day. The distribution chamber in 1926 then split the delivery into two destinations, to the north and to the south. The northern system (capacity approximately 5–6 million gallons per day) went to Alabama Street via a 36-inch pipe and then to the northern portion of Bellingham along pipes that roughly paralleled Alabama Street. The southern system (capacity

---

[*] Ibid.

approximately 5.5 million gallons per day) went via a 30-inch pipe to what was then called Lake Street (now Lakeway and Holly Streets) and on into town. A connection between the two systems was first established with a 12-inch pipe at the juncture of Alabama/Yew Streets (northern system) and Lake/Woburn Streets (southern system). From there, a maze of pipes delivered water to all of Bellingham, and many more interconnections between the northern and southern systems tended to equalize pressure and serve as backup connections should any part of the system fail.

Citizens continued to be concerned about the quality of the water from the lake (sophisticated filtration and chemical treatment were unavailable), so for a time, swimming was prohibited in the lake, starting in 1906 and ending in the 1930s when enforcement was simply no longer pursued. Little did the authorities realize that human activity around the lake—with its attendant pollution—was about to increase with the development and expansion of Silver Beach, White City, Geneva and Blue Canyon. Furthermore, regulations were enacted that forbade ships from dumping pollutants, like toilet waste, into the lake. Later, the problem of lakeside septic tanks would need to be addressed.

For years, the maintenance of the level of the lake was disputed. Many dams had been constructed at the outflow of Lake Whatcom—some legal, some not. The FLC had built one in the late 1880s. Another was erected in June 1896. In 1899, a law was passed allowing the construction of a dam at the outflow of the lake. The $3,000 cost was to be shared equally by the FLC and the City of Whatcom. Not all transpired quickly. When the dam was finally completed in 1906, the cost to the city was $64,000, not the $1,500 it could have originally been. This dam was built in part to avoid the flooding that occurred periodically. In April 1911, the city of Bellingham constructed a different and more substantial dam at the northwest end of the lake where it drained into Whatcom Creek. Legal struggles regarding the level of the lake ultimately ended in the Washington State Supreme Court ruling that the water level could be no higher than 314.94 feet above sea level. Currently, the level of the lake is raised and lowered a maximum of 2.5 feet as conditions dictate.

Other sources had historically provided water for the Fairhaven/Bellingham/Sehome/Whatcom complex. Lake Padden was the origin of water for Fairhaven ("South Bellingham"), beginning in about 1890. In January 1890, a 6-mile pipe was begun from Lake Padden to Fairhaven, under a 50-year franchise to the Fairhaven City Water Company. Lake Padden was above the city by 437 feet (Lake Whatcom was 315 feet above mean tide level), so this system was also completely gravity-fed. It was finished in March 1890. This privately owned system, named the Fairhaven City Water and Power Company, was subsequently purchased by the City of Bellingham in 1925 for $165,900, and it remained in place and functioning until 1968. In 1926, the average citizen used 100–150 gallons of water per day. The Lake Whatcom system delivered about 6–9 million gallons of water per day, while the Lake Padden system sent 1.5–3 million gallons per day to Fairhaven. One foot of elevation or diminution in the level of water in Lake Whatcom held 1.5 billion gallons, while in Lake Padden, one foot of depth held 40 million gallons. Natural outflow from either lake was lowest in the months of August, September and October. An analysis projected that the natural flow from Lake Whatcom could ultimately supply 200,000–300,000 persons with adequate water.

By the late 1930s, it became clear that the water supply for Bellingham was in peril. Unregulated and unmonitored sewage discharge around Lake Whatcom was fouling the drinking water for the city. One large sewage line even dumped its effluent in the lake near the intake for the drinking water. Waste from the Bloedel-Donovan lumber mills was still clogging the water delivery system. Divers occasionally needed to descend into the lake to clear the inlets of waste from the lumber processing: sawdust, wood chips and other byproducts of the mills' activity. In the face of these problems, citizens were willing to pay for improvements to the water plant.

Now water from Lake Whatcom comes from an intake located near Geneva just south of Watkins Point on the western shore of the lake. The conduit for delivering water to the Bellingham treatment plant today begins as a 1,250-foot wooden pipe that runs from the intake 40–44 feet below the surface of Lake Whatcom near Watkins Point in Geneva. The construction of this system was approached in stages. Stage 1 included the construction of the control dam at the outlet of Lake Whatcom into Whatcom Creek. Stage 2 involved the building of the intake in Lake Whatcom, the tunnel from the lake to the water treatment plant in Whatcom Falls Park and an industrial water line to the Puget Sound Pulp and Timber Company's plant at Bellingham Bay (which could also be available for other industries as they developed). Stage 3 was the construction of a connection from the Nooksack River to Lake Whatcom. Cost estimates in 1937 were thought to be staggering at the time: the total approached $750,000. Even as these projects were being considered, Bellingham residents were required to boil water for drinking and cooking because the existing water treatment was inadequate, making the need for the new system even more urgent and contributing to the eventual passage of the bond issue. In 1937, Bellingham was using about 20 million gallons per day for all purposes: residential, commercial and industrial. The voters approved this project in December 1937.

The conduit from the intake in the lake to the "tunnel gate house" at the edge of the lake was to be a 1,250-foot, 72-inch-diameter cast-iron pipe. (The intake was called a tower, though it was completely underwater.) Many alternate sites were considered, but the location off Watkins Point proved to be the best balance of cost and function. Engineers designed the intake so that an extension of the pipe southeast toward Ramona Park could be added in the future if new data showed any advantage to this alternate position. By October 1939, the design had reverted to a wooden pipe (it was projected to "last indefinitely under water").*

Original estimates placed the length of the concrete-lined tunnel needed from the edge of the lake to the treatment plant at about 7,850 feet. It was to be a slightly oval or horseshoe-shaped structure, 6 x 6.5 feet in diameter. The tunnel was begun in March 1939. The geology was favorable, and construction proceeded. The tunnel/pipe was a cast-in-place concrete-lined construction. The tunnel as finally constructed is 7,560 feet long from the lake to the screen and chlorine house in Whatcom Falls Park near the fish hatchery. The tunnel slope is only 0.1 percent, descending from 298.5 feet at the intake to 290.94 feet at the Whatcom Park end of the pipe—thus completely gravity-fed. This tunnel was completed in 1939, though the connection to the city's water service main was not achieved until September 1940. Initially, the Georgia-Pacific Pulp and Paper Mill used two-thirds of the water flow, but it phased out its use over the years 2001 to 2007. Lake water analysis revealed that with the substantial decrease in the volume of water used by Georgia-Pacific, Lake Whatcom's water quality deteriorated. The large volume of water used by Georgia-Pacific had actually served to "flush" the lake and purify it. The speed of the water flow within the cast-in-place concrete tube lining is now about one foot per second. The pipe has the capacity for about 100 million gallons per day, though currently it conducts an average of 10–16 million gallons per day, with a peak daily usage of about 20 million gallons per day. The average usage at the paper mill had been about 30–50 million gallons per day, and now, for only human use, it ranges from 10 to 20 million gallons per day. Puget Sound Energy uses about 1 million gallons per day. A rather large volume of water is lost to leakage, estimated to be up to 5 million

* *Bellingham Herald*, July 8, 1940.

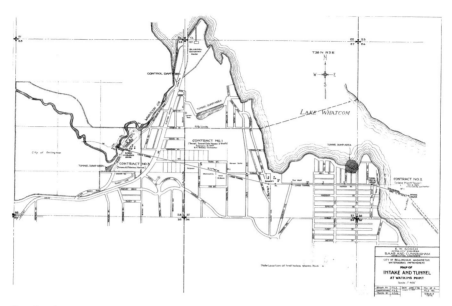

Details of the course of the Lake Whatcom Water Tunnel directed to the water treatment plant, completed in about 1940. The original name of the street intersection where the gatehouse is located was Marion at Grand; today, these streets are named Lakeway Drive and Lake Whatcom Boulevard. The tunnel courses westward from the gatehouse under Geneva Elementary School to Euclid Park, then on to the screen house next to the fish hatchery. *Appendix A, Map of Intake and Tunnel at Watkins Point, City of Bellingham, Lake Whatcom Tunnel Condition Assessment Report, July 2015.*

gallons per day. Overall, on average over the year, the tunnel delivers about 16 million gallons of water per day.

The first proposal to divert some of the flow from the South Fork of the Nooksack River to Lake Whatcom was made in December 1899, though it was decidedly premature, and similar construction did not happen until many years later, although from the Middle Fork. In 1961, the city of Bellingham, in a cost-sharing project with the Georgia-Pacific pulp mill, began connecting the Middle Fork of the Nooksack River to the south end of Lake Whatcom by a dam and a water pipe. The dam was about 25 feet tall and 150 feet wide, and it was completed in 1962. The route taken by the water diverted in this manner was through a 1.6-mile tunnel through Bowman Mountain and a 9.5-mile pipe through Acme Valley. It emptied into Mirror Lake, then drained to Lake Whatcom via Anderson Creek.

In the late 1990s, environmentalists began claiming that the dam was detrimental to the chinook salmon, steelhead and bull trout that used this river for spawning and by affecting salmon, it secondarily impacted whales.

Water system construction, 1940. The intake of the pipe was placed at a depth of 44 feet where the lake is 53 feet deep, about 1,250 feet from shore. Pictured here is the beginning of the tunnel at Watkins Point, looking toward the west. This structure is the gatehouse under construction. *Whatcom Museum, 2011.0040.000003.*

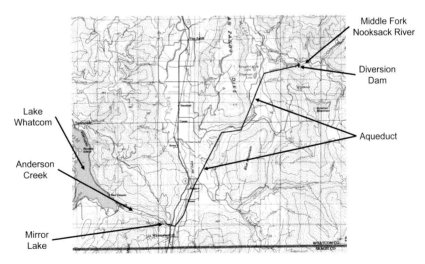

Piping from the Middle Fork of the Nooksack River to Mirror Lake; water then flows to the south end of Lake Whatcom. *Figure adapted from United States Department of the Interior, Geological Survey, Bellingham Quadrangle, 1:100,000. Washington, 1975.*

In 1999, the Environmental Protection Agency declared the salmon to be an endangered species, so the push heightened to remove the dam. It was removed in 2020, and the origin of the water diversion into Lake Whatcom was altered so that the dam was no longer necessary. The intake for the water destined for Lake Whatcom was moved to the south bank of the Middle Fork of the Nooksack, located about seven hundred feet upstream from the dam that was removed. The intake structure had a screen to keep fish from being swept to Lake Whatcom, and it did not inhibit the movement of fish in this area.

A dam is still present at the outflow of Lake Whatcom near Electric Avenue. It controls the level of the lake. Today about half the water that flows into Lake Whatcom comes from precipitation and runoff from the watershed; about half comes from the diversion from the Nooksack River. The outflow is about 78 percent to Whatcom Creek, 11 percent to the City of Bellingham water supply, 8 percent to evaporation and 3 percent to the fish hatchery. The average time for any unit of water entering the lake until it exits is 7.4 years.

Lake Whatcom provides about 11 million gallons of treated water daily to the one hundred thousand residents of Bellingham and Whatcom County. Before 2007, another 33 million gallons daily of untreated water were used daily by the Georgia-Pacific plant located on Bellingham Bay, which was provided by a separate pipe to the plant on the bayfront. When the Georgia-Pacific plant completed its closure in 2007–08, that amount of water became available for other uses, and the draw from Lake Whatcom decreased.

Currently, the water treatment plant, built in 1968 and upgraded in 2018, can handle 24 million gallons of water per day. The water first goes from Lake Whatcom Basin No. 2 near Geneva by gravity feed through a 1,200-foot wooden pipe to the "gatehouse." It then travels through a tunnel to the "screenhouse" located in Whatcom Falls Park. There, larger debris is removed, and the water passes on to the next location of the water treatment plant near the park. There, it undergoes a dissolved air floatation system, an alum mixing station and a chlorination system. It is again filtered and sent to a 1-million-gallon reservoir called the Clearwell, where it is again chlorinated and passed to the Contact Time Reservoir, itself capable of holding 16 million gallons. As the water exits this reservoir, yet another chlorination process is completed, and it is sent throughout the city, where 410 miles of main piping deliver it to over one hundred thousand customers in the Bellingham area who are downstream from over ninety distribution sites. Storage tanks hold more than twice the daily needs for the city, so adequate reserve protects the city from any shortage. Average water usage is 8 million gallons in the winter and 14 million gallons in the summer. Current use is about 11 million gallons daily, so the entire system could theoretically support twice the population.

A second supplier of water uses Lake Whatcom as its source. In 1968, the Lake Whatcom Water District No. 10 began piping water from Lake Whatcom's Basin No. 3, just north of Reveille Island, purifying it and distributing it to Sudden Valley, Geneva, South Bay and part of Northshore. It is capable of processing 425,000 gallons of water daily to be delivered to 1,800 customers, mostly in Sudden Valley. Its intake is a one-foot-diameter pipe located at a depth of 70 feet approximately 315 feet from shore.

Furthermore, about 250 homes around the lake take water directly from the lake itself, and a few smaller public water systems do the same.

Water volume is not the only issue affecting Lake Whatcom. Phosphorus, algae, invasive aquatic species, benzene, toluene, xylene and other substances that degrade water quality are equally important to the health and utility of the lake. They are monitored constantly.

Chapter 16

CONCLUSION

Lake Whatcom has had a storied past. Its future lies in the maintenance of the lake as a water source, both for drinking and for recreation. Communities continue to prosper, though the coal, timber and large amusement centers are gone. The many parks around the lake contribute to the high quality of life for local residents.

Early Lake Whatcom Timeline

Event	Date
First White settlers	1852
Geneva town platted	1887
First steamboat (*Geneva*) operational on Lake Whatcom	1888
Silver Beach town platted	1890
Silver Beach Hotel opened	1891
Blue Canyon Mine opened	1891
Blue Canyon town founded	1891
First coal transported from Blue Canyon Mine	1892
Trolley from Bellingham to Silver Beach opened	1892

Event	Date
Bellingham Bay & Eastern Railroad completed to Blue Canyon	1892[1]
Blue Canyon Mine disaster	1895
Larson Lumber Company founded	1901
Bellingham Bay & Eastern Railroad sold to Northern Pacific	1902[2]
Bellingham formed from four cities	1903
White City opened	1906
Bloedel-Donovan Lumber Mill founded	1913
White City closed	1916
Blue Canyon Mine closed	1919[3]
Silver Beach Hotel closed	1922[4]
Trolley system closed	1938
Current water piping system from Lake Whatcom completed	1940
Bloedel-Donovan Park dedicated	1948[5]
Northern Pacific Route to Blue Canyon closed	Circa 1954[6]
Sudden Valley development platted	1969

[1] The railroad was not completed entirely from Bellingham to Blue Canyon until January 1902.

[2] October 1902.

[3] The mine was officially closed in 1919, but the last mine shaft was closed in 1921.

[4] The hotel became a dormitory for coal miners in 1922; it was essentially abandoned in 1924 and demolished in 1930.

[5] The land was donated in 1946 but not dedicated until 1948.

[6] Abandonment of this railroad line was disputed in court for over forty years.

BIBLIOGRAPHY

Benoit, Matt. "Remembering Bellingham's Forgotten 'White City' Amusement Park." *Whatcom Talk*, November 11, 2019.

Bickerstaff, Alison. "What Lies Beneath Bellingham Attracts Attention of Federal Government." *Whatcom Watch Online*, March 2003.

Biery, Galen. Galen Biery Papers and Photographs, 1861–1992, especially Boxes 2, 4 and 10. Archives West, Center for Pacific Northwest Studies. Western Washington University, Bellingham, WA.

Blumenthal, Richard W., ed. *The Early Exploration of Inland Washington Waters: Journals and Logs from Six Expeditions, 1786–1792*. Jefferson, North Carolina: McFarland, 2004.

Bureau of Land Management. General Land Office Records. U.S. Department of the Interior.

City of Bellingham. "Aerial Photos." https://cob.org/services/maps/aerial.

Clark, Donald H. *18 Men and a Horse*. Seattle: Metropolitan Press, 1949.

Edson, Lelah Jackson. *The Fourth Corner: Highlights from the Early Northwest*. Bellingham, WA: Cox Brothers, 1951.

Erickson, Eric. *Whatcom County Washington Logging and Lumber Index: 1852 to 2005*. Maple Falls, WA: Black Mountain Forestry Center, 2005.

Fitzhugh, E.C. *Annual Report of the Commissioner of the U.S. Indian Affairs Office for the Year 1857*. Report No. 135, June 18, 1857, Bellingham Bay Agency, Washington Territory. Washington, DC: William A. Harris, 1858. https://search.library.wisc.edu/digital/AIV4K4ANELCH2R8T.

Friday, Chris. "Geology and Ecology of Whatcom Creek." Western Washington University, 1999. https://bellinghamblog.files.wordpress.com/2014/05/geology-ecology-of-whatcom-creek.pdf.

Griffin, Brian L. *The Donovan Diaries*. Bellingham, WA: Knox Cellars Publishing Company, 2020.

———. *Treasures from the Trunk: The J.J. Donovan Story*. Bellingham, WA: Knox Cellars Publishing Company, 2013.

The Ham: An Eclectic History of Bellingham, Washington (blog). https://hamtopia.wordpress.com.

Historic Map Works. www.historicmapworks.com.

"How Blue Canyon Coal Came to New Whatcom." Spiers and Anderson, Printers, New Whatcom, WA, June 1892. Folder 70, Box 38, Series 12: Whatcom County 1890–2003, Subseries 1: Whatcom County, Pamphlet Collection, 1893–2003, Center for Pacific Northwest Studies, Western Washington University, Bellingham, WA.

Jenkins, Olaf Pitt. *Geological Investigation of the Coal Fields of Western Whatcom County, Washington*. Bulletin No. 28 (Geological Series), State of Washington, Division of Geology, Department of Conservation and Development. Olympia, WA: F.M. Lamborn, 1923.

Jentges, Cecil W. *Images of America: Bellingham*. Charleston, SC: Arcadia Publishing, 2015.

Jewell, Jeff. "Silver Beach Hotel: A Lakeside Resort in 1891." *BBJ Today, The Bellingham Business Journal*, January 31, 2008.

———. "Silver Beach Hotel Led a Checkered Life." History at a Glance, *Whatcom Magazine*, n.d.

Journal of the Whatcom County Historical Society.

Koert, Dorothy, and Galen Biery. *Looking Back: The Collectors' Edition. Memories of Whatcom County/Bellingham*. Grandpa's Attic, Bellingham, Washington, 2003.

Lookout Mountain Forest Preserve and Lake Whatcom Park Recreational Trail Plan. Whatcom County Council Resolution No. 2016-040. Whatcom County Parks and Recreation. June 2016. https://www.whatcomcounty.us/DocumentCenter/View/23920/Lookout-Mountain-Forest-Preserve--Lake-Whatcom-Park-Recreational-Trail-Plan.

Moen, Wayne S. *Mines and Mineral Deposits of Whatcom County, Washington*. Bulletin No. 57, Division of Mines and Geology, Department of Natural Resources, State of Washington, Olympia, Washington, 1969. https://www.dnr.wa.gov/Publications/ger_b57_mines_mineral_dep_whatcom_1.pdf

Moore, F. Stanley. *An Historical Geography of the Settlement Around Lake Whatcom Prior to 1920*. Technical Report No. 21. Institute for Freshwater Studies, Western Washington State College. June 1973. Folder 64, Box 39, Series 12: Whatcom County 1890–2003, Subseries 1: Whatcom County, Pamphlet Collection, 1893–2003, Center for Pacific Northwest Studies, Western Washington University, Bellingham, WA.

Mustoe, Gordon. "Coal Mines of Whatcom County." YouTube video, presented to the Whatcom County Historical Society on November 13, 2014. https://www.youtube.com/watch?v=2wJXogtElAY.

Peterson, Becky. *The Lake Whatcom Watershed: A Retrospective Resource Directory Companion Report, 1850–2007*. Geneva Consulting, March 2008. www.cob.org/documents/pw/lw/lake-whatcom-history.pdf.

Polk, R.L. & Co's Bellingham Directories. Archives West, Center for Pacific Northwest Studies, Western Washington University, Bellingham, WA.

Roth, Lottie Roeder. *History of Whatcom County*. Vols. 1 and 2. Chicago: Pioneer Historical Publishing Company, 1926.

Sanborn Fire Insurance Maps. Library of Congress and Archives West, Center for Pacific Northwest Studies, Western Washington University, Bellingham, WA.

Scott, James William, and Daniel E. Turbeville III. *Early Industries of Bellingham Bay and Whatcom County: A Photographic Essay*. Bellingham, WA: Fourth Corner Registry, 1980. Archives West, Center for Pacific Northwest Studies. Western Washington University, Bellingham, WA.

Silver Beach Neighborhood Association. *2010 Silver Beach Neighborhood Plan*. Bellingham, WA: City of Bellingham, 2010. https://cob.org/wp-content/uploads/silver-beach-cc-proposed-plan.pdf.

Skagit River Journal of History and Folklore. http://www.skagitriverjournal.com.

Thomson, R.H. "Report on Present City Water Supply and Probable Future Requirements." City of Bellingham, Washington, December 31, 1926. Folder 5, Box 40, Series 12: Whatcom County 1890–2003, Subseries 1: Whatcom County, Pamphlet Collection, 1857–2003, Archives West, Center for Pacific Northwest Studies, Western Washington University, Bellingham, WA.

Turbeville, Daniel E., III. "The Electric Railway Era in Northwest Washington, 1890–1930." Thesis and Occasional Paper No. 12. Archives West, Center for Pacific Northwest Studies, Western Washington University, Bellingham, WA.

Vonheeder, Ellis R. *Coal Reserves of Whatcom County, Washington*. State of Washington, Department of Natural Resources, Division of Geology and Earth Resources, May 1975. https://www.dnr.wa.gov/publications/ger_ofr75-9_coal_whatcom_co_62k.pdf

Warger, Todd. *Shipyard*. Bellingham, WA: Village Books, Chuckanut Editions, 2023.

Whatcom County Tax Parcel Viewer https://whatcom.maps.arcgis.com/apps/webappviewer/index.html?id=f2f8eaa500b04f54948c680bb280129f.

Zobrist, Elaine L. *Ghost Towns of Lake Whatcom*. Bellingham, WA: Self-published, 1979. Revised 2002.

Newspapers: CPNWS

Bellingham Bay Express
Bellingham Blade
Bellingham Daily Times
Bellingham Herald
Bellingham Reveille
Fairhaven Herald
Lynden Pioneer Press
Lynden Tribune
Seattle Daily Times
Seattle Post-Intelligencer
Seattle Republican
Sehome Morning Gazette
Whatcom–New Whatcom Reveille
Whatcom Reveille

ABOUT THE AUTHOR

H. Leon Greene is a retired cardiologist and emeritus professor of medicine at the University of Washington. Author of hundreds of medical scientific papers, over thirty book chapters and four previous books, he lives in Silver Beach, one of the areas surrounding Lake Whatcom. His interest in history now extends to the description of his own neighborhood.